THE GREAT
CIRCUS
TRAIN WRECK
OF 1918

THE GREAT CIRCUS TRAIN WRECK OF 1918

TRAGEDY ON THE INDIANA LAKESHORE

RICHARD M. LYTLE

THE
History
PRESS

Published by The History Press
Charleston, SC 29403
www.historypress.net

First published 2010
Second printing 2013

Manufactured in the United States

ISBN 978.1.59629.931.3

Library of Congress Cataloging-in-Publication Data

Lytle, Richard M., 1947-
The great circus train wreck of 1918 : tragedy on the Indiana lakeshore / Richard M. Lytle.
p. cm.
Includes bibliographical references.
ISBN 978-1-59629-931-3
1. Hagenbeck-Wallace Circus. 2. Railroad accidents--Indiana--Hammond. I. Title.
GV1821.H3L97 2010
363.12'20977299--dc22
2010021444

CONTENTS

PREFACE

In 2005, the Suzanne G. Long Local History Room of the Hammond Public Library, a local history research center operated jointly by the library and the Hammond Historical Society, began investigating the possibility of reprinting and once again publishing the original account of the terrible incident that was the subject of Warren A. Reeder Jr.'s book, *No Performances Today*. The inquiry stemmed from telephone calls made to the Hammond Public Library's Local History Room to determine if copies of Reeder's book were on hand and could be purchased. Once a number of those questions had been received, permission to either reprint or rewrite the book was sought from the Reeder family.

The following facts contributed to the decision to create this edited version: 1) North State Press no longer exists; 2) the only copies of Reeder's book available to the public are part of the library collection; 3) new primary source material regarding some victims of the tragedy has recently come into the hands of the Hammond Historical Society; and 4) additional secondary sources of material exist that have not previously been utilized, and additional research on some of the participants has taken place.

After receiving the blessing of the Reeder family members, I began the work of researching, editing, writing and publishing this update to the story. Hopefully, you will find it an interesting look back at a distant moment in time and a fragmented view of Americana that has all but vanished.

ACKNOWLEDGEMENTS

This book is dedicated to the memory of several people: Warren A. Reeder Sr. (1883–1947), who was unable to take Junior Reeder to the circus that fateful day of June 22, 1918; Janet Virginia Reeder (1954–1960), who dearly loved circuses but wanted to see Jesus; and Warren A. Reeder Jr. (1913–1976), past president of the Hammond Historical Society and trustee for the Hammond Public Library. He was the one who originally told this story in his 1972 publication, *No Performances Today*.

As was true when Warren Reeder first wrote this story, no one person can compile a book of this type without the assistance and contributions of others. One of the contributors to this effort was Nancy Masten, archivist of the Miami County Museum in Peru, Indiana. Another was Mr. Tom Dunwoody of Peru's Circus Hall of Fame. A special thank-you is also owed to librarian Carol Williams, of the Hammond Public Library, who proofread this work and offered helpful suggestions. Further recognition must go to Mrs. Florence Hammond Cleveland, Mrs. Katherine Thiegze and Mrs. Suzanne G. Long, my predecessors in the Suzanne G. Long Local History Room, who helped gather the locally generated material used in this account.

Chapter 1

THE HAGENBECK-WALLACE CIRCUS

By 1918, the name of Ben E. Wallace had stood out in the circus world for more than thirty years. In fact, it had stood out since before 1886; that was the year the "Great Wallace Show" took to the rails for the first time.

Although technically a veteran of the Civil War, Wallace was not a combat soldier. He was an eighteen-year-old bounty soldier, a hired substitute for Robert F. Effinger, who was enrolled on February 28, 1865, into Company K of a reorganized Thirteenth Indiana Volunteer Infantry Regiment then encamped at the west edge of the government center for LaPorte County. A little more than four months later, shortly after arriving at New York Harbor, Wallace was discharged from Federal service and returned home.[1]

That home was a growing community named Peru, the center of local government for Miami County, Indiana, and it was becoming a bustling railroad transportation hub. It was also adjacent to the nonreservation lands owned by members of the Miami Indian tribe who remained on individually owned farms after the majority of the tribe members had been forced westward nearly twenty years earlier.

Once back in Peru, Wallace soon developed a modest and growing horse-trading business, which, by 1881, he was advertising as "the largest livery stable in Indiana." Author Nancy Newman, in an article that appeared in the local newspaper about one hundred years later, wrote about how Wallace got into the circus business:

> *In 1882, Wallace, who had been interested in circuses for several years, attended a sale of equipment of the W.C. Coup show. The large railroad show had passed through Peru on its way to Detroit. Heavily mortgaged, it could not meet its financial obligations and was declared bankrupt.*
>
> *Wallace returned from the sale with six or seven rail cars full of tents, poles, costuming and other equipment. He attended a sale for another show in Texas, returning with several rail cars of horses. He purchased other animals in Chicago, and in December he contracted with a local firm, Sullivan & Eagle, for construction of some ornate wagons.*[2]

Throughout 1883, Wallace continued to build up his circus by hiring the best performers he could find. Finally, after recovering from a late January 1884 fire that killed some of his exotic animals, the first Wallace Show gave its inaugural performance in Peru and then went bravely forth in the spring of 1884.[3]

Traveling as a horse-drawn road show, the Wallace and Co.'s Great World Menagerie spent most of its time in southern Indiana, Ohio, West Virginia and Kentucky and, quite possibly to the amazement of all its investors, returned a sizable sum. After another successful tour in 1885 that saw the one-ring show traveling in a procession of twenty-six wagons, Wallace made the decision to expand his next performance route throughout the nation. He also decided to change its name. Consequently, in 1886, the Great Wallace Show took to the rails and traveled by train for the first time.[4]

Ben Wallace had an eye for good horseflesh, and by 1886, he was considered one of the top horse experts in the country. He also had the gift of showmanship. Within a few years, his Great Wallace Show grew from a mere fifteen cars to more than forty freight and wagon carriers that held a massive big top tent, a menagerie tent, two horse tents, the sideshow tent, a cookhouse and various sleeping quarters for the performers.[5]

The Wallace Winter Quarters were located on an old farm that was once owned by Gabriel Godfroy, son of the last Miami Indian chief to

Right: A young Benjamin Wallace.
Courtesy Miami County Museum.

Below: One of the original
wagons of the Wallace Show.
Courtesy Miami County Museum.

The Wallace Show bandwagon. *Courtesy Miami County Museum.*

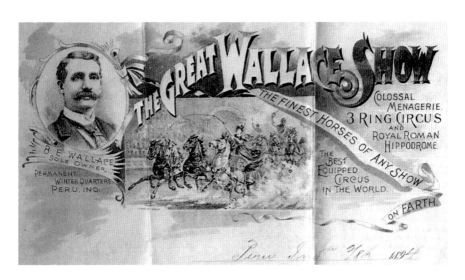

An 1894 flyer for the Wallace Show. *Courtesy Miami County Museum.*

live in Indiana. Wallace bought the 220-acre farm when Godfroy lost the ability to have the farm counted as part of the Miami Indian tribal lands. It was the state and local tax assessed on the property that forced that sale. Wallace bought the Godfroy property in 1892 and continued buying other farmlands (there were several other Indian farms nearby in the same situation) until he owned all land on both sides of what is now Indiana State Route 124 all the way to the eastern edge of Peru, Indiana, a distance of two miles. The Godfroy Farm and the other farms nearby, situated on the north side of the Wabash River at the confluence point where the Mississinewa River joins the Wabash, were notorious not only for being some of the best crop-producing acreage in the area but also for being subject to annual floods.

Finally, in July 1892, the law of averages caught up with the Great Wallace Show. After logging thousands of miles on the nation's ribbons of steel, the Wallace Show experienced its first railroad train wreck. Twenty-six of the Wallace Show's highly prized, performance-schooled horses, worth a total of at least $5,000, were killed.[6] The Show would spend a lot of money and months of training to replace them.

Eleven years later, at the town of Durand, Michigan, fate again caught up with the Great Wallace Show. On August 7, 1903, the show train was arriving at the local rail yard after having been conveyed from its departure point as two separate train sections. The first train section, traveling several minutes ahead of the second section, was safely in the Durand rail yard. The second circus train section did not slow down as it approached and entered the yard at its regular traveling speed. It slammed into the rear of the first section, killing twenty-six men, including the trainmaster, and an unknown number of railroad employees. Several animals were also killed. The engineer of the second section later claimed that his air brakes failed even though subsequent testing revealed that they were in perfect working order. This would become the second worst circus train wreck ever.[7]

By some adroit legal maneuvering, the details of which are still not clear, in 1907 Ben Wallace obtained the famous animal circus of Carl Hagenbeck, Chicago's version of New York City's P.T. Barnum show. The price reportedly paid was $45,000, truly a princely sum in that day and age. Immediately, Wallace changed the name of his show to

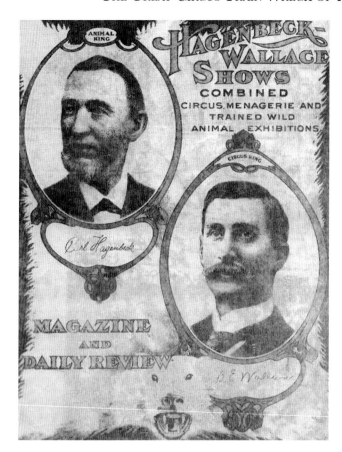

A 1914 advertising insert of the combined Hagenbeck-Wallace Shows. *Courtesy Miami County Museum.*

the Hagenbeck-Wallace Circus and began advertising the show as the "world's highest-class circus."[8] In truth, it may actually have achieved that classification, for it was ranked beside both the Ringling Brothers and the Barnum & Bailey Circuses. The size of the augmented circus in 1907 required that it travel as two completely separate train sections, with each section numbering at least twenty-eight rail cars.

Evidently, Carl Hagenbeck was not very happy with Ben Wallace's business reputation. Some people have since claimed that Wallace's philosophy was, perhaps, best summed up in an admonition he gave to his employees, "Shoot square as long as you are in Peru." True or not, the man who spent his first eighteen adult years as a horse trader in Peru desired, and got, the respect and honor of his hometown.[9] What he thought about the opinion of the rest of the world is now unknown.

Despite a 1908 lawsuit filed by Hagenbeck in the courts of Cook County, Illinois, the combined show remained the Hagenbeck-Wallace Circus for evermore. And the newest version of the Hagenbeck-Wallace Circus was no nickel-and-dime affair either, even though Wallace made his living off those nickels and dimes. According to one of Peru, Indiana's newspapers (most likely the *Peru Republican*), at the end of 1907, after Ben Wallace had bought out the interests of three other partners for $125,000, the Hagenbeck-Wallace show was completely owned by Wallace and John Talbot of Denver, Colorado.[10]

That was the way things stood until the latter part of March 1913, when the advent of a spring storm system proved devastating to the Midwestern states drained by the Ohio River. Marked by a massive tornado that caused widespread destruction in Omaha, Nebraska, the storm system continued eastward up the Ohio River Valley, dropping two inches of relatively warm rain on the snow-covered and frozen ground of southern Ohio and Indiana. The rain and melted snow could only drain off into the lakes, creeks and smaller rivers, pushing the Miami and Wabash Rivers, which

The departure parade of the Hagenbeck-Wallace Circus in Peru, Indiana, 1909. *Courtesy Miami County Museum.*

The departure parade passing Ben Wallace's house in Peru, Indiana, 1909. *Courtesy Miami County Museum.*

eventually received that runoff, well beyond flood stage. Newspaper reports of between two and five thousand deaths in Dayton, Ohio, and between two and four hundred deaths in Peru, Indiana, were printed on March 26 and, even today, still testify to the severity of the overall situation.[11]

Fortunately, those newspaper reports would prove to be incorrect, at least as far as the deaths of Peru citizens were concerned, but the overall effect of the flood was very costly nonetheless. Ben Wallace and his family actually did not live on the winter quarters grounds (he had an imposing home in Peru), but a good many men did live on the grounds, and seventy-five of them were trapped on the property by the floodwater. The location of Wallace's home did not prevent him from being trapped, however. The floodwater was knee-deep around his house, and he, like every other city resident, sought shelter on the upper floors of whatever second-story building was available.

Several days would pass before a firm estimate of the flood damage could be made. Finally, on March 29, the reports that the Wabash River had dropped nine feet in Peru and would be completely gone by that night, along with another that the death list had a total of twenty-eight people, were sent to all newspapers. However, those reports would not begin to list the costs of the damages to individual homes, business or industries in

The Chesapeake & Ohio Railroad depot, two miles downstream from the Peru Winter Quarters, where a drowned elephant lay after the 1913 flood. *Courtesy Miami County Museum.*

and around all of the affected cities. Later, it was reported that damages to the Hagenbeck-Wallace Circus would total over $150,000. That figure included the loss of eight elephants; one of the dead elephants was found lying next to the Chesapeake & Ohio Railroad station some two or three miles downstream.[12]

While Hammond and the other towns within the Calumet River drainage area were largely spared from flooding, they were still subject to other types of drama. For instance, on March 30, 1913, just one day after the crisis peaked in the middle of the state, an event occurred that had little meaning to most newspaper readers but would eventually become a subject of some consideration five years later. In the late afternoon, a Michigan Central passenger train arrived at its Hammond, Indiana station with a dying engineer at its controls. The evening newspaper reported the event as follows:

> *More than a hundred passengers on a Michigan Central train, bound*
> *from Kalamazoo, Mich., to Chicago, rode several miles at top speed*

Saturday evening drawn by an engine with a dying and unconscious man at the throttle…As the train pulled into Hammond, with the fireman driving the engine with one hand and holding the engineer propped up in his seat with the other, the sufferer's painful breathing stopped… His form relaxed in death as the wheels stopped moving, and a second later the white-faced fireman staggered out of the cab and called for assistance. John Bently was the engineer. The fireman, Joseph Gondert, and the conductor of the train, Edward Hurley, carried the body into the Hammond waiting room. The train was delayed half an hour while the coroner was taking Gondert's statement.[13]

Still, the big news in the Indiana newspapers continued to be the flood and the recovery efforts being made as the water receded. In community after community all over the state, reports of the pick-up and cleanup efforts were being printed for the next several days. It was not an easy task, and it did not happen very quickly, but the flooded homes, businesses and communities were soon back to normal. So, too, were Ben Wallace and his circus. After repairing damaged wagons and equipment, and after renting other exotic animals to replace those that drowned, the Hagenbeck-Wallace Circus still managed to begin its yearly performance tour on schedule. However, the financial burden of recovery from the flood appears to have persuaded Wallace to sell out to Edward M. Ballard of French Lick, Indiana, in June 1913.[14]

Actually, there were other partners in the new venture: Mr. Jerry Mugivan and Bert Bowers. Also reputedly associated with Ballard were two famous Hoosier political figures: a man named Crawford Fairbanks, who was a brewer in Terre Haute, and Thomas Taggart, who was the operator of a famous spa at French Lick. Mr. Taggart was powerful enough to wangle the vice-presidency of the United States for Thomas Marshall in 1912. Together these men formed the American Circus Corporation and soon came to own quite a few other circuses in addition to the Hagenbeck-Wallace Circus.

By the beginning of the 1918 performance tour, the multiple circuses owned by the American Circus Corporation were unquestionably big business in terms of both income and expense. Because of the risk involved in transporting such large bodies of people, equipment and

Mr. Ed Ballard. *Courtesy Miami County Museum.*

livestock on a daily basis, no syndicate, partnership or individual dared undertake the gamble without the protection of a corporate shield. Gone were the days when a single owner, like Wallace, could rely on the income of just one traveling show. It now took the combined income of many traveling shows, each under a hired manager, to turn an annual profit.

In 1918 the manager of the Hagenbeck-Wallace Show was Charles A. Gollmar, and the advance man for the show was his brother, Fred C. Gollmar. The brothers Gollmar were two survivors of four brothers who had formerly owned their own circus, and many of their old troupers had followed them to the Hagenbeck-Wallace Circus. In years past, the Gollmar Show had appeared in many of the same communities that were on the Hagenbeck-Wallace 1918 performance schedule, so the brothers were not strangers to the business or that year's route.[15]

Circuses did not normally repeat their routes each year. Customers would grow tired of repetitive acts, so they alternated with one another, not out of politeness but because of sound and shrewd business reasons. The 1918 schedule reflected that philosophy, and with good reason. Generally speaking, the city of Hammond, Indiana, had been good to the Hagenbeck-Wallace Circus.[16]

Initially, though, Hammond had not proven to be an ordinary experience for the circus. At the first appearance of the Hagenbeck-Wallace Show on August 24, 1907, the elephants refused to cross an iron truss lift bridge over the Grand Calumet River that connected the north and south parts of Hammond's Calumet Avenue. To the great glee of the local newspaper, the elephants forced the all-important circus parade to deviate from the exact parade route decreed by city officials who issued the parade permit. According to the *Lake County Times*, it was the city administration's introduction to "the most magnificent production that ever paid a visit here."[17]

Three years after that appearance, the Hagenbeck-Wallace Circus returned to Hammond. And once again, on August 1, there was an opening-day incident:

> *The middle of the morning parade in 1910 also saw a disturbance. A local young man, later to become a prominent attorney and upright law-abiding citizen of the community, became insistent that he be allowed*

his clean shirts at the Chinese laundry located on Hohman Avenue at the dog-leg.

"No tickee—no washee," he was imperturbably informed.

Events that followed are a bit hazy at this late date, but in the ensuing battle he reputedly "chased four Celestials from their place of business," not appreciating the hot iron he had dodged and which broke the window.

Someone yelled "Fight!" A slightly deaf and overly eager citizen thought the call was "Fire!" He pulled the fire alarm box and the excitement of the parade was broken for a while by the charge of horses pulling the steaming fire equipment to the scene. It was quickly cured and the police soothed over the incident.[18]

Another visit came on July 22, 1912, and passed in a less riotous but more unsavory manner. Evidently, traveling circuses attracted a great many drifters and pickpockets, although the managers discouraged such associations. In fact, traveling circuses were so popular that a certain criminal element followed them from place to place, something that prompted the *Lake County Times* to print the following warning when it learned of the 1912 play date: "LOCK YOUR WINDOWS AND FASTEN YOUR DOORS BEFORE YOU GO TO THE CIRCUS."

Unusual incidents occurred during the 1912 play date. Local newspapers reported that a Mrs. Hartman almost lost her necklace when it was quietly cut from her back during the parade. Fortunately for her, a spectator saved it. After the evening performance on the circus's first night, a Mrs. John Beach, one of the bareback riders, was trapped under a C&O freight train before the horrified eyes of hundreds of onlookers as she and her husband were strolling toward the downtown part of the city. Fortunately, although the train dragged her a considerable distance, she emerged with only a few scratches.

That year the local newspaper sadly estimated on the day after the show departed that "$10,000 had been taken out of Hammond by the circus." That was just the box office net figure. Probably a lot more money than that had been drained from the town citizens.[19]

Newsworthy incidents aside, the show's management quickly realized that the steady growth of Hammond and its surrounding communities on

Circus members' typical traveling attire of the day. *Courtesy Hammond Public Library.*

both sides of the Indiana-Illinois state line meant eager crowds and good profit margins. The area was a favorite of many other circuses as well, some of which played across the Illinois state line in West Hammond, now Calumet City, Illinois.

July 28, 1914, was an ominous day for the Hagenbeck-Wallace Circus. Austria declared war against Serbia that day, setting in motion political and military forces that helped to force events four years in the future.[20] And although no one could foresee it in 1914, the show would not schedule another appearance in Hammond for four more years.

Chapter 2

CALUMET REGION RAILROAD DEVELOPMENT

There are many communities within the United States that owe their existence to the railroads, and Hammond, Indiana, is one of them. Tucked into the extreme northwest corner of the Hoosier State, Hammond has come to be considered by many as an out-of-state extension of metropolitan Chicago. In some ways, it has always been so, but in other ways, it really was Indiana's last frontier.

The honor of being the first residents within the area immediately south of the lower tip of Lake Michigan goes to the Indians who inhabited the land they called *Calumet*. The Calumet region of those days was essentially an expanse of sand ridges separated by swamps, all of which were part of the drainage system for the Calumet River. It was a drainage system wholly contained within the region, as it originated near the eastern edges of the ancient limits of Lake Michigan, wandered west well into what became Illinois and then turned back eastward through the region to drain into Lake Michigan itself. The westward-flowing part of the river farthest to the south became the Little Calumet, while the eastward-flowing part of the river, which provided some natural drainage to the Illinois swamps and was thus larger in size and greater in volume, traversed the region farther north and became the Grand Calumet. In the later years of the nineteenth century, the natural flow of the river would be forever altered by engineering projects in Illinois that would

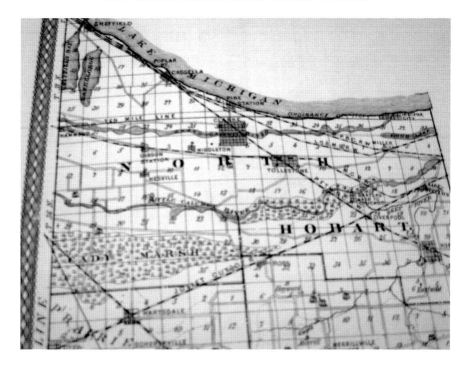

The northwest corner of Indiana in the 1870s. Note the absence of several cities that have subsequently developed in the area. *Courtesy Hammond Public Library.*

create an artificial connection to Lake Michigan within that state. That new connection reversed the flow of Indiana's portion of the Grand Calumet so that both the Little Calumet and the Grand Calumet Rivers drained into the Chicago waterways.

Initially, it was topography that dictated the earliest commercial development within the Calumet region. Other than the very low sand ridges, the overall topography was flat swampy ground covered with hardwood trees and scrubs that, when drained, made for good farming. Consequently, once the Indians were moved west of the Missouri River and the ground opened to homesteading, the first permanent settlers were largely immigrant German farmers.[21]

Prior to 1851, most of those settlers had yet to arrive in the extreme northwest corner of Indiana. In fact, the Michigan Central Railroad reached what would eventually become the center of the region when there were fewer than one hundred people living in the area. When that railroad stopped at what it called West Point, the end of track at the time, is still a bit hazy. Records suggest it was sometime between 1849 and 1851, but exactly what day, month and year remains unknown.

What is known is that sometime in 1851, Ernst and Caroline Hohman decided to buy a forty-acre homestead located where the old stagecoach road to and from Chicago crossed the Grand Calumet River. They were quickly followed by Joseph Hess and his wife, who arrived at West Point that same year and opened a restaurant for the construction and work gangs, as well as railroad passengers traveling between Detroit and Chicago. A few years later, Hess started a little cluster of farms and shops located one mile south of West End, which would eventually be known as Hessville.[22]

In that early period, the only other community cluster was a village named Tollison, which was centered on the Gibson family homestead and located some four or five miles east of the Hohman homestead. That was where Michigan Central trains connecting the region with the eastern United States began and ended their journeys; that is, until 1852, when rail connections into Chicago were completed.

The Michigan Central Railroad was not the only rail line being built to Chicago, however. In fact, it was not the first to actually reach Chicago. That honor belonged to the Michigan Southern Railroad, which was building its line of track much closer to the Lake Michigan shoreline. In its wake (it reached Chicago in 1852, three months ahead of its competitor), another small cluster of residents along the lakeshore was created and became known as Whiting's Crossing.

It was from those little villages that the cities of Gary, Hammond and Whiting would grow. Many years later, the City of Gary annexed Tollison, and the City of Hammond annexed Hessville. The City of Whiting, as it became known, was able to fight off annexation efforts and remained autonomous. From all of them, though, other cities developed: East Chicago, Merrillville, Griffith, Highland, Schererville, Munster and the city once known as West Hammond and now called Calumet City, Illinois.

Six years later, a third railroad entered the Calumet Region on its way from Pittsburgh to Chicago. Actually named the Pittsburgh, Fort Wayne and Ohio and later commonly known as the Pennsylvania Rail Road, it angled in from the southeastern part of the region and proceeded to the Lake Michigan shoreline in 1858. The "Pennsy," as it would eventually be called, laid its rail nearly side by side with the Michigan Southern trackage, where it crossed the Illinois state boundary.

In 1860, the population census for Lake County, Indiana, totaled 9,145 people, with 729 men, women and children of all ages residing in North Township. Only twelve families then lived within what would one day be the city limits of Hammond. Almost all of them were farming families, and the produce they sent into the Chicago markets would represent the single biggest contribution the region could make once the American Civil War started.[23] Throughout that war and for several years thereafter, the region seemed destined to remain an agricultural activity center that happened to contain some significant swamps. The railroads did bring a few new people into the region, but the overall effect was negligible.[24]

Over the years, Ernst Hohman and his wife had made themselves a good living out of their homestead. Ernst had built a bridge over the Grand Calumet River and turned his frontier cabin into a hotel that could accommodate anyone traveling to and from Chicago on the old stagecoach road between that growing city and all points south and east. The trains still only stopped at Tollison, but considering the large swamps to the northeast and south, the only practical road for wagons and horsemen still passed by his farm and over his bridge. The Hohman Farm was more than just forty acres, too. By the end of the Civil War, Ernst and Caroline's property had grown to more than four hundred acres, and they had been joined by Caroline's sister's family, the Sohls, who had another large farm on the south side of the Grand Calumet and the Michigan Central tracks. The Sohls operated a small general store at their homestead for several years, and between the two families, that was the sum of all commercial activity in the region west of Hessville. All in all, Hohman's Bridge, as the tiny community was known, had about a half-dozen farming families, supplemented by an equal number in Hessville and perhaps two or three more families living in the Whiting area by Lake Michigan.

And then, all of that changed.

On September 1, 1869, four men riding in a buckboard wagon arrived at the Hohman homestead. Two of the men, George H. Hammond and

Caleb Ives, were from Detroit. David B. Plummer, the third man, was a cattle buyer associated with Chicago's Union Stockyards. The fourth man, Marcus M. Towle, was a new associate of the three men and most likely the one driving the carriage. The men were conducting a survey of the region in search of a good location to start a new business venture, and they were looking for some very specific features. First, the site chosen had to be on or very close to a railroad. Second, it had to be near sources of large quantities of ice, and most important of all, it had to be low in cost. The business they would create would be a large-scale slaughterhouse, and their plan was to ship freshly killed and butchered beef and other meat products to major East Coast markets in the middle and northeastern states. Already they had a contract in operation for the construction of ten new railroad cars specially designed to allow a new method of shipping fresh meat. Now, they just needed a facility to produce the product.

On the south end of Hohman's Bridge, they found what they were looking for. Between the bank of the Grand Calumet River and the tracks of the Michigan Central Railroad was enough available land to begin the operation, all owned by Ernst Hohman. Fifteen acres were purchased, and a young Marcus Towle was placed in charge of constructing the buildings and supervising the butchering operation. Within a month, work had begun: three rail cars loaded with cut lumber were delivered to the site; eighteen men were brought from Chicago to build the buildings and begin the kill operation; a rail spur onto the site was laid; and the new refrigeration cars, now commonly called reefers, arrived. Then came the cattle and ice, and by the end of the year, the George H. Hammond Packing Company was in business. The total investment split between Hammond, Ives and Plummer at that point was a mere $6,000 for the land, reefers, cattle, buildings, ice and manpower to make it happen.[25]

Supervisor Towle and the 18 men he brought into the region represented a significant increase in the local population, but they were not the only new residents in the area. The next federal census revealed that the overall population in North Township had more than doubled to 1,507 people. Evidently, then as now, the lure of new business and money was the only attraction, as there was absolutely no other reason for such a rapid increase. There was some real money flowing into the meatpacking business, too. The volume of dressed meats flowing out of the area quickly reached and then exceeded four railroad carloads each day, Sundays included. As of May 4, 1871, the firm had spent $336,720 for cattle, and the figures reported on July 8 of that year put the firm's cash balance at $266,081. By 1873, two years later, the Hammond Meat Packing Company passed the $1,000,000 annual sales mark and was anticipating further increases in business orders once the quality of shipping refrigerated dress beef was fully accepted and more eastern markets opened.[26]

Getting workers to hire on at the packinghouse was not all that hard, but keeping them there was a real challenge. From the very beginning of the slaughterhouse construction, there had been a housing shortage, a situation that remained for many, many years. Even though Towle had a boardinghouse built for his workers that his wife ran for quite some time, the shortage continued. Initially, in the budding community only the most basic of services, food and shelter were available. Soon, though, the usual frontier saloons began appearing, along with other stores of various kinds. By 1873, Marcus Towle had fifty-two men working seven days a week.[27] That same year, Towle petitioned the United States government to establish a post office and was then appointed to serve as the first postmaster. Initially referred to as State Line Slaughterhouse, Indiana, the name was soon changed to Hammond in honor of the meatpacking company's owner. The following year, the first spin-off business, a glue and fertilizer factory, was created on the Illinois side of the state line in what became West Hammond.[28]

In 1875, another railroad, the Baltimore and Ohio, was built around the southern tip of Lake Michigan, which also passed into Illinois and the southern section of Chicago. That was the same year that Marcus Towle decided to draw out the original ground plat for what would eventually become the unincorporated village of Hammond. In 1880, that village became a fact, and for the first time in history, it was so designated in the census conducted that spring. By then the village had grown to include about seven hundred men, women and children of all ages—with four hundred of them being male and three hundred, female. All of this indicated the changes taking place in the economic and social development of the entire region.[29]

The 1882 arrival of three additional national rail carriers—commonly called the Nickel Platte, the Erie and the Monon, entering the village from the south and southeast—essentially guaranteed that Hammond would grow into a city. All three of those new railroads crossed the Michigan Central rails at nearly right angles in the relatively small space between the slaughterhouse to the west of the combined right of way and the south end of Hohman's Bridge over the Grand Calumet to the east. Farther to the east, beyond the south end of that bridge, was the Hammond Lumber Company, which, at that time, was supplying the lumber being used to build the community. Each of those three new railroads established important rail yards where maintenance shops existed and freight was transferred from train to train or railroad to railroad. Those facilities meant jobs and people who would stay to become part of the community—people who would need homes and all the rest of the consumer services normally demanded.

The Hammond Lumber Company was first started by Marcus Towle, and in 1876, it was purchased by Mr. Jacob Rimbach, who had been the track maintenance supervisor at West End for twenty-two years. Rimbach was married to a good German woman who had given him four daughters. It is assumed that the girls did not have much trouble attracting suitable young men, but they must have been ready to move

The city of Hammond, as seen from the roof of the Hammond Packing Company Building, circa 1890. *Courtesy Hammond Public Library.*

to a more metropolitan place than West End. Consequently, when Towle approached Rimbach about taking over the Lumber Company property, and Rimbach heard the fantastic deal Towle was willing to make, the agreement was quickly made. Soon afterward, another German family, headed by Gottlieb Muench, decided to sell their farm in Hessville and move the three miles to the village of Hammond, where they joined the Rimbachs. Mrs. Rimbach and Mrs. Muench then put their heads together, secured the assistance of Mrs. Hohman and laid an ultimatum on Mr. Rimbach, Mr. Muench and Mr. Towle. Their battle cry was "Sixteen Saloons and No Church!" Thus, the campaign to bring a church to the village was begun.

Two years later, with Hammond counting a village population of 2,960 people, and with religious and commercial services sufficient to support that number, the more influential citizens of the population, with Marcus Towle at the forefront, began the process of having the village incorporated under Indiana law as a city. That way, the civil service positions of mayor and governing city council members, as well as a city marshal's office and a volunteer fire department, could be created. Once that process was complete, the time came for the new city to hold its first election. Marcus Towle was elected as Hammond's first mayor—a result that did not surprise anyone.[30]

By 1884, the new city of Hammond had three rail yards and a multitude of passenger and freight stations where just ten years earlier there had only been one yard and one small station. All of those facilities were within one or two miles from where the old stage road, now called Hohman Avenue, was bisected by the Michigan Central tracks and the rails of the Erie, Monon and Nickel Platte Railroads. That traffic congestion point, which included foot traffic, horse and wagon movement and the addition of an unbelievable number of trains, was being controlled by two switching towers. The largest was the State Line Tower with its two hundred mechanical switching levers. Those switches controlled all east- and westbound rail traffic. The State Line Tower was the second largest of its kind in the world,[31] and it definitely was the largest railroad control tower on the North American continent. The second tower was built by the Erie & Lackawana, and it was located much closer to the rail intersection where the four railroads crossed one another. Typically, it

A modern-era picture of the Hohman Avenue switching tower in Hammond, Indiana—a close copy of Ivanhoe Tower. *Courtesy Hammond Public Library.*

A modern-era picture of State Line Tower, the second-largest switching tower in the world. It was demolished in October 2000. *Courtesy Hammond Public Library.*

was known as the Hohman Avenue Tower and served as a satellite facility to regulate all north- and southbound traffic through that intersection.[32]

George Hammond died on December 29, 1886, at the early age of forty-eight and left his estate to his widow and their eleven children. The property he had in Indiana came under the operation and management of appointed corporate officers who eventually sold it to foreign investors. These investors brought different methods to the company's freight rate negotiations with the Michigan Central Railroad.[33] One of those new methods was the creation of short-line rail systems, called beltway railroads, which allowed the easy movement of rail cars from one railroad (and any of its spur lines to manufacturing plants) to other railroads operating within the Chicago region. The standardization of railroad operating methods, control signals and space separating track rails was what made that new type of rail operation possible.[34]

The Elgin, Joliet and Eastern Railroad was probably the first of the new beltway rail systems to appear in the Greater Chicago area. It arrived in Hammond in 1888 and laid its tracks along the north bank of the Grand Calumet River. That inspired the corporate syndicate controlling the George H. Hammond Packing Company to join in the creation of the Chicago, Hammond & Western Belt-line Railroad, which connected the packinghouse facilities in Hammond and West Hammond with all other major national rail carriers that served the region.[35]

Seeing the advantage and profit potential of beltway rail operations, Marcus Towle decided to get into the business. He was one of the partners who created the Chicago & Calumet Railroad in 1891. This railroad interconnected John D. Rockefeller's oil refinery, located on the shore of Lake Michigan north of Hammond. Located a short distance east of the village of Whiting, Rockefeller's Standard Oil Company of Indiana was just completing its initial phase of construction and production and was ready to begin the shipment of oil and gasoline via rail. Towle built his Chicago & Calumet Railroad so that crude oil and refined product output sent to and from the refinery could be shipped on any rail carrier connected to the Chicago rail network.[36]

By the time the 1890 census was taken in Hammond, the George H. Hammond Company, at that point of time the premier industry in the Calumet Region, had a workforce exceeding 1,000 men and women who were getting an annual payroll of over $500,000. That year's census revealed that the Indiana population residing within walking distance of the packinghouse included 5,428 men, women and children of all ages, races, colors and creeds.[37] The city named after the packing plant owner had an even fifty streets with its political, local government and business center within sight of the packinghouse entrance and the Michigan Central Railroad station. Additionally, on the Illinois side of the state line, another community of about 700 people, who were all tied to the Hammond Company in one fashion or another, had developed and was calling itself West Hammond.[38] Thirty-four years later, that Illinois village would rename itself Calumet City.[39]

As the entire region advanced toward the beginning of a new century, the industrialization of the southern tip of Lake Michigan, on both sides of the now invisible state boundary, brought expansion and population growth at even higher rates. The decade of the 1890s brought a major rail-intensive steel mill to the Lake Michigan shore immediately east of the oil refinery, as well as the Wabash Railroad. The City of Hammond benefitted from the new activity, both directly and indirectly, by annexing all land between the Grand Calumet River and a point ten miles out into Lake Michigan itself. By that action, every rail line that passed eastward from Chicago within a distance of fifteen miles from the shore of that Great Lake had to pass through the city of Hammond. However, the rationale behind the annexation was not about trains and passengers; it was about securing an inexhaustible source of fresh water to support a growing population.[40]

At nearly the same time, the Michigan Central, the oldest railroad through the region, became part of the conglomerate New York Central, and before the end of the decade, both the Chicago, Hammond & Western and the Chicago & Calumet Trail operations were also acquired. Beginning in about 1896, the New York Central system lumped the two beltway companies with some of the old Michigan Central trackage and created a new rail company called the Indiana Harbor Belt, which still exists. One old part of the new Indiana Harbor Belt was the original marshaling yard, West Point, which seems to be a surprising addition to the new company—but it really was not. The New York Central system was then the controlling stockholder of the

Indiana Harbor Belt, and the change in designated usage allowed the yard to serve as a major rail car interchange hub for all east–west traffic of all the northeastern rail carriers.

The construction of the Chesapeake & Ohio Railroad through the area in 1902 essentially completed railroad development in the northwest corner of Indiana. The only exception was the building of the South Shore Electric Railroad, which connected the Indiana communities being developed in the one-hundred-mile distance between South Bend, Indiana, and Chicago. That electric rail line began in 1908 as a commuter operation, and even though it claimed to have a freight capability, passenger traffic was its main source of revenue.

Chapter 3

THE CIRCUS IS COMING

The 1918 performance schedule for the Hagenbeck-Wallace Circus was a typical version of the average annual tour routine. Opening at Cincinnati, Ohio, on April 26, the show moved in a northeasterly direction through Pennsylvania and New York and into the New England states. Then it turned west, pausing among the large and small industrial cities of upper New York State and the Canadian provinces. After that, the show was set to return back to the United States and hop along the major cities in northern Ohio and lower Michigan before stopping to give performances at Michigan City and Hammond, Indiana. After the evening show in Hammond, it was set go to Monroe and Beloit, Wisconsin, and then move on to Minnesota and the Dakotas. From there, the show was scheduled to backtrack through upper Minnesota and Wisconsin again and then drop southward into Illinois, Iowa and southern Indiana. It would end in a grand-finale engagement on the Chicago lakefront in late September.[41]

Circuses were not generally prosperous in 1918. Labor shortages and the high taxes on admission tickets caused by the United States' participation in World War I, the Spanish influenza epidemic then sweeping the nation and an all-out war-production effort being made by both the United States and Canada were considered to be negative influences that subtracted from the average annual tour profits. Of course, the overall negative influences on the 1918 income expected would not be measured until after the performance schedule was concluded. But only one month into that schedule, financial indicators were already becoming noticeable. On June 15 of that year, an article in *Billboard Magazine*, a popular trade publication, further expanded on the rationale behind complaints of low profitability. The article said that the new Daylight Savings Time was having an adverse effect: "The night shows start late; the sideshows are affected, and all combined, getting off the lot is later." Motion pictures, though silent and still in their infancy as an industry, were also cited as a "deterrent to business." However, the magazine did add that "business was good."[42]

Ed Ballard claimed to have an investment of $3,000,000 in the Hagenbeck-Wallace Circus, and that claim was probably fairly accurate. Carried by fifty-eight rail cars owned by the circus and moved as special trains by the several railroads it relied on, the circus had twenty-two tents and one thousand employees on the weekly payroll, which amounted to $7,500 per day. This did not include other overhead expenses, such as feeding and transporting a group of roustabouts and artists led by the famous Rosa Rosalind, who, as a star member of the cast, reputedly drew $25,000 per year. There were other major performers drawing top wages as well: Marcelline Cevene of the Cevene Sextette who was a lithe, young and beautiful tightrope walker; the Cottrell-Powell English bareback riders; the famous Flying Wards of the high trapeze act; and the astounding Von Ritter, who stood on his head and slid down the tight wire stretched from the peak of the big-top tent to the ground below. All in all, the Hagenbeck-Wallace Circus went on tour with twenty-five different acts and was advertising the presence of sixty aerialists, sixty acrobats, sixty riders, fifty clowns and "100! Count them, 100 dancing girls!" Added to that impressive pool of performing talent were the show's seven elephants, lions, tigers, zebras, camels, a hippopotamus, hundreds of draft horses, perhaps as many as eighty horse-drawn wagons and twenty specially trained trick ponies. Those numbers indicated the unique spectacle that the Hagenbeck-Wallace Circus of 1918 offered to the young, old, rich and poor who lived in or near the cities it traveled through.

Every year the advertising effort for a scheduled Hagenbeck-Wallace show was extensive and very coordinated. Typically, an "advance car"

The Cottrell-Powell English bareback riders. *Courtesy Circus Hall of Fame.*

under the direction of J.E. Eviston would come into a town about three weeks prior to a performance with its own crew. That crew of twenty-two billposters, six lithographers and Mr. Floyd King, who was a press agent under Eviston, would quickly cover a thirty-mile radius around the show grounds to attract customers. One week before the performance, a second advance car, called an "excursion car," arrived with Mr. J.W. Nedrow in charge, seconded by press agent P. Robinson, and wound up the publicity effort. "A glittering three-mile parade" was promised, and considering the sheer size of the overall operation, that promise was usually kept.[43]

Operationally, the circus conducted each year's performance tour much like a military campaign. The "advance" and "excursion" cars were the circus equivalent to military scouting parties operating ahead of the main show. The main show itself traveled in two different train sections, with about twenty-five rail cars in each section. The first section, carrying all the animals and livestock, was equal to a forward military element that would establish the most basic essentials for each

The Flying Wards; Mayme Ward is the second girl from the right. *Courtesy Miami County Museum.*

campsite—the cook's tent and the various picket lines needed to house, feed and groom the livestock. Then all hands would help erect the rest of the camp once the second section arrived. When that second section did appear, those animals were immediately put to work unloading the newly arrived wagons and equipment and all of the other gear required for the afternoon performance. Next came the amazing task of erecting tents, especially the huge big top, which was accomplished with a practiced skill rarely seen elsewhere. With that work done, the animals, wagons and performers were then dressed and formed into the marching parade, which would travel through the community and lead everyone to the circus grounds.

To say that daily life and order in the Hagenbeck-Wallace Circus was run on a caste system much like a military organization was not an exaggeration. Circus administration and owners traveling with the show lived in private cars or compartments nearest the middle of the train. The cars of the performers were next, with some cars having private compartments for starring family performing acts and regular upper and lower berths for single performers and other senior staff members. This custom automatically shifted the less skilled workers and roustabouts into the last one or two sleeping cars. Generally, those in the same department ate and slept together and essentially operated as an ad hoc family circle within the larger circus community. Considering that the show traveled from one performance location to another every day of the week except Sundays, the entire system had long ago been developed into a fast, efficient and profitable routine. In fact, it was so fast, efficient and profitable that, in later years, the United States Army would go and study the different methods circuses used in order to develop the procedures needed to move large mechanized forces on military campaigns.

The packing, unpacking and constant jostling and handling of tents, wagons, railroad cars, canvases, seating, ropes, poles and pulleys meant constant wear and tear on property on which the circus depended.

Unloading the circus somewhere in Vermont. *Courtesy Miami County Museum.*

Serviceable and highly portable modern equipment was a basic operation expense, and Ed Ballard, owner of the Hagenbeck-Wallace Circus, realized that the expectations of wartime audiences required a new tent, new seating and a new lighting system. Fortunately, those components had already been ordered when the show reached Michigan City, Indiana, on Friday, June 21, 1918. Ballard normally accompanied the circus and was with it when it arrived in Michigan City, but instead of staying though the show, he continued on to Chicago, where he intended to complete delivery arrangements for a new tent purchased from the U.S. Tent and Awning Company. He planned to bring the new tent back to the main part of the show once it was settled in Hammond. After the regular Saturday evening performance, the show would stay in Hammond through Sunday, June 23, and the roustabouts, working under the direction of Whitney Oldknow, the superintendent of canvas, would reroll the new big-top tent so it would be ready for use in Monroe, Wisconsin.

The Michigan City performance was a charity show for the inmates of the Indiana State Penitentiary held in the afternoon of June 21, and it was not followed by the usual evening show. That meant that the circus would have a light day and would be able to make a more leisurely jump to its next scheduled city. Even as the last acts were going through their routines that afternoon, the process of putting the show back on its train cars was begun. Once all the tents were down, rolled and placed on carriage wagons and those wagons moved to the makeshift loading ramps, the task of putting the wagons, all caged animals and other boxed equipment onto the rail cars commenced.

There were six sleeper cars plus all of the Hagenbeck-Wallace animals and their handlers making up that first circus train section. It departed Michigan City at 1:00 a.m., heading west on the old Michigan Central Railroad tracks. It would first go through Hammond and then on to Union Stockyards in South Chicago, where the animals could be easily fed and watered before being returned to Hammond. The second circus train would meet the first in Hammond. Except for the New York Central Railroad engine, its accompanying tender and the obligatory New York Central caboose, all of the rail cars were old, wooden-framed, limited-service rolling stock owned by the Hagenbeck-Wallace Circus. By decree from the federal government, the overall condition of that rolling stock, though still legal to operate on the nation's rail system, required that all circus train equipment be limited to speeds of twenty-five miles per hour or less.

That first circus train was passing through Hammond when the second circus train departed Michigan City, Indiana. That last departure occurred at about 2:30 a.m. on June 22, 1918. Designed by the New York Central Railroad as Extra 7826, this train was drawn by Engine 7826 and consisted of seven stock cars, followed by fourteen flatcars carrying the gilt-covered circus wagons and trucks painted in Hagenbeck-Wallace yellow. Next came the four old sleeping cars that the circus had purchased from the Pullman Car Company. The last rail car was the New York Central caboose occupied by a brakeman. Like the first circus train section, that second train was also restricted to speeds under twenty-five miles per hour.

Train conductor R.W. Johnson, an employee of the New York Central, was in charge of Extra 7826, and riding with him in the caboose was trainmaster Fred Whipple, also from the New York Central, acting as overseer for both circus train sections. The third man riding in the caboose was rear brakeman Oscar Timm. Locomotive engineer Gasper, fireman Clyde Phillips and front brakeman Curtis Aust were up front in the cab of the steam engine as a routine part of their job. Brakeman Aust's additional duty was to periodically look back over the following cars and judge their operating condition.

While still legally serviceable, all of the Hagenbeck-Wallace-owned railroad cars were made almost entirely of wood. Neither the cars—stock or flat—nor the coaches had steel sills under them. R.W. Johnson, the conductor of the second section of the circus train, later testified that "the only iron or steel I saw about these circus coaches was the trucks, the frame of the trucks and one vestibule. The rest was all wood."[44] Even the rebuilt Pullman sleeping cars were of light construction. Steel cars had existed for over a decade in 1918, and even the Pullman Car Company had completed the transition to the new construction material. In fact, the Hammond stop for the circus would be near the second manufacturing location of the Standard Steel Car Company headquartered close to Pittsburgh, Pennsylvania.

As for the coaches themselves, they were all thirty or more years old and long ago removed from the active Pullman roster. Predominately, all of the sleepers were built between 1881 and 1885, used on the nations premier passengers routes and then retired from further service about twenty years later. (A general dating of the coaches is possible from the size of the journal bearings used on each axle. They were the 1869-recommended standard three and three-quarters by seven inches as opposed to the 1889 standard of four-and-a-quarter- by eight-inch journal bearings. In 1918, modern rail equipment used a standard of five-and-a-quarter- by nine-inch bearing).[45]

Sold to a rebuilding company in Indiana between 1900 and 1905, the coaches had been reconditioned to acceptable standards and were again sold to the Hagenbeck-Wallace Circus for exactly the purpose for which they were being used. Overall length of the sleeping cars varied from fifty-eight to seventy-two feet, with the smaller cars containing one or two separate compartments. Sleeping accommodations in the longer cars generally had been converted into a bunk-type configuration that stacked the occupants two and, in some cases, three high. Of the four sleepers in the second circus train, only one had electrical lighting. Nighttime visibility in the other three cars depended on overhead kerosene or coal oil lamps.[46]

The military-style circus caste system was fully evident in the sleeping accommodations allotted to each individual. With Ed Ballard absent from the show, command of the entire Hagenbeck-Wallace Circus was in the hands of general manager Charles Gollmar. His stateroom, which was also occupied by his wife, was in the first sleeping car. Also in that leading car were many of the family acts and some of the single female performers. More single and married couples without children were in the next sleeper, while the last two cars in front of the caboose berthed many of the male canvas handlers and roustabouts. Of course, it was a warm June night, and the heat in those densely berthed sleeping cars—during an era well before the advent of air conditioning—encouraged a number of the lowly handlers and roustabouts to find sleeping space in the wagons and trucks carried on flatcars ahead of the sleepers.

The dispatch board of the Michigan City marshaling yard for the New York Central gave the departure time of Extra 7826 as 2:30 a.m.

but was uncertain of the exact time the second circus train cleared the yard. The train still had to be assembled, and the caboose, New York Central #2109, had to be attached to the rear before it could actually begin its westward journey. Once Extra 7826 was on its way, Engineer Gasper held the speed of his train somewhat below its allowed rate all the way to a slight rise in elevation named East Gary Hill. During the run westward, the engine headlight died. Slowing down for the climb over the hill anyway, Gasper dropped the speed even lower than usual so that he could climb to the front of the engine and place another lantern in the lamp case—a tricky task even during perfect daylight conditions.

Gasper maintained a reduced speed of about ten to twelve miles per hour as the train passed through Gary and then picked up the speed to about eighteen miles per hour as the train went by the Tollison Switching Tower. The tower operator there recorded the time of Extra 7826's passage as being 3:44 a.m. He immediately got on the telephone and called the next tower operator three miles west on the right of way and notified him of the circus train's approach to the Ivanhoe switch.[47]

Sometime during the previous twenty or so years, another small belt-line operation named the Gary & Western Railroad had added a third east–west set of rails that paralleled the Michigan Central trackage about twenty feet to the north. In addition, sometime during the preceding thirty years, the Elgin, Joliet & Eastern Railway (EJ&E) had built a single north–south track that crossed both the old double-tracked east–west main line of the original Michigan Central and the single track of the Gary & Western (G&W) at a ninety-degree angle. By 1918, the Indiana Harbor Belt Railroad had ownership of the G&W and was using it as the easiest path to route trains through its Gibson Yard facilities and to manufacturing industries in Hammond on the north side of the Grand Calumet River.

The Interlocking Tower at Ivanhoe was located just west of the point where the EJ&E crossed the dual tracks of the old Michigan Central. The distance from Ivanhoe Tower to the Michigan Central Depot in Hammond was only five and a half miles, and the intended performance ground for the show was within walking distance of that depot. Inside the tower were thirty-three manually operated switching levers that controlled the track connections to the G&W, as well as the EJ&E crossover. Those switches were electrically connected to automatic signaling systems that applied to both the EJ&E and the old Michigan Central rights of way. The entire West Division of the New York Central, which included the old Michigan Central but did not include the EJ&E, was completely equipped with modern automatic block signals. They all were of the upper-quadrant, three-position, daytime-indicator type that used red, yellow and green lights as nighttime indicators.[48]

The average length of the signal block was about one mile in each direction from the tower. Battery-powered direct-current electrical circuits were used, and these were connected so that the signal caution position was shown for each track switch unless it was overridden by the electrically controlled clear signal. The manually thrown levers in the tower actually moved the switch rails from one track connection to another, and those rails "completed" the electrical circuits controlling the signal indicators. Automatic signal 2581 served as the distant block boundary signal for westbound traffic approaching Ivanhoe Tower and the EJ&E crossing. That signal was about 5,360 feet east of what was called the home signal bridge for Ivanhoe. The "home signal bridge" was itself about 950 feet east of the tower. A matching set of signals on another bridge for all eastbound traffic on the old Michigan Central was similarly located at the western end of the block. The tower operators at Tollison and Ivanhoe were talking to each other about the proper setting of these levers during the time that Extra 7826 traveled between the departure signal for Tollison Tower and the approach signal for Ivanhoe Tower.

The destination of the Hagenbeck-Wallace Circus was the north side of the Grand Calumet River, near where some of Hammond's busiest manufacturing facilities—Betz Medical and Surgical Supply Company for example—were located. Naturally, Extra 7826 had orders to take the G&W branch connection and change tracks as it approached Ivanhoe Tower. To make that change, Engineer Gasper began dropping the speed of his train down to about six miles per hour as it rounded a slight curve east of the switch and passed by the Ivanhoe approach signal. That signal, as well as the Ivanhoe home signal, was showing the proper clearance indicators for the transition over to the G&W trackage.[49]

It was at that point when fate intervened.

Brakeman Timm was taking a good look at the north side of his train cars as they moved slowly through the curve, and he could plainly see the blaze of a hot journal box located in the middle of the train. It turned out to be a flatcar with "Hagenbeck-Wallace number 72" painted on its side. Conductor Johnson was immediately told, and both men lit fusees to use for signaling purposes; Johnson used his to give Engineer Gasper a stop signal. While he did that, Brakeman Timm dropped off the caboose to go back eastward on the tracks and post danger warnings for any rail traffic behind them.

Up in the locomotive cab, Engineer Gasper lightly applied his air brakes as his engine made the transition from the southernmost of the Michigan Central tracks, through the northernmost track and onto the G&W track. He stopped his train about seventy feet east of the EJ&E crossing, either unaware or unconcerned that the last few cars of his train were still on the westbound Michigan Central track. Then Gasper, expecting to soon get a proceed signal, set the independent brake for his engine and released his automatic air brakes before looking back along the south side of his train.[50]

Chapter 4

HELL ON WHEELS

The New York Central Railroad system was always busy with normally scheduled and nonscheduled traffic. The wartime needs of the United States' participation in the world war made it even busier than usual. In June 1918, the need to move U.S. Army troops from their training camps to ports of embarkation was paramount, and the New York Central served as a major source of eastward transport for troops destined to serve in the American Expeditionary Force fighting in France. Once the troop-carrying rail cars were unloaded, they had to be returned westward to be used for the next batch of soldiers ordered overseas.

Like the circus train, Extra 8485 was the leading half of a two-part train of empty troop carriers. Drawn by a standard New York Central main-line locomotive numbered 8485, a "ten-wheeler" 4-6-0-configured steam engine with an equally standard coal and water tender, the train was bringing twenty-one empty steel-constructed Pullman sleeper cars, owned by the Canadian Pacific Railroad and borrowed for moving U.S. troops, from Kalamazoo, Michigan, back to the Chicago area.

The man in charge of Extra 8485 was actually another train conductor with the last name of Johnson. He was conductor L. Johnson and was completely unrelated to the second circus train conductor. The rest of the crew on Extra 8485 when it left Kalamazoo included engineer Alonzo Sargent, fireman Edward F. Burgess, a brakeman named W.R. Jackson, flagman J.E. Moyer and three porters. Only Engineer Sargent remained in the cab of locomotive 8485 throughout the entire trip. Because the train had fairly modern equipment and was completely empty of all passengers, most of the crewmen were in the caboose. Conductor Johnson was the only person who moved freely about his train.[51]

Engineer Sargent lived in Jackson, Michigan, and departed his home on New York Central Train 41 at about 5:00 p.m. on June 21. He had not slept prior to his departure, and he didn't have much chance to sleep once he reached Kalamazoo. At about 8:00 p.m., he was called to take the throttle on Extra 8485; he did get a chance to eat prior to reporting to his train. Sargent's train section was dispatched out of Kalamazoo at 10:15 p.m. and actually left the Kalamazoo yard at 10:55 p.m. All along the right of way from Kalamazoo to Michigan City, Indiana, Extra 8485 followed a slow freight that evidently had some problems because Sargent had to halt his train twice between the southwestern Michigan communities of Dowagiac and Niles due to danger signals.

According to Conductor Johnson's watch, the empty troop train arrived at Michigan City at 2:47 a.m. on the morning of June 22, 1918, stopping at the Michigan City yard standpipe, where Fireman Burgess was relieved of further duty with the train. Another man, fireman Gustav Klauss, took that place in the locomotive cab, while Sargent monitored the intake of water into the tender.

At 2:57 a.m., Engineer Sargent had Extra 8485 moving on the route to East Gary at a speed fluctuating between twenty-five and thirty miles per hour with the belief that he had a clear track all the way. That idea was deceptive; the interval between his train and Extra 7826 was only fourteen minutes when he passed through the Porter signals. However, the question of whether anyone on Extra 8485 knew that the circus train was in front of the troop train remains unanswered.

At the approach signal to the East Gary block, Sargent first spotted a caution signal that indicated a train ahead and obediently reduced his train's speed. The signal changed to all clear before his engine passed it by, so Sargent kept going; still, he reduced his speed to about ten to fifteen miles per hour as he went through Gary.

Sargent picked up speed to about twenty miles per hour when he passed into the Tollison signal block, as all the indicators he saw were clear. At the west end of the Tollison signal block, Sargent later stated that he saw the caution signal displayed but that he expected the right of way ahead to clear momentarily as it had earlier on his trip. That was Sargent's first mistake. Once in the mile-long space between the Tollison block and the next one, the Ivanhoe block, Sargent again picked up the speed of his train to about twenty-five miles per hour, never realizing he was now only eight minutes behind the slower circus train.[52]

The space between Tollison and Ivanhoe Towers is about three miles. Each tower's block signal system begins and ends about one mile from its respective tower, leaving a one-mile "dead" space between the two sets of signal blocks. Reports later indicated that a strong wind was blowing southward off Lake Michigan, and between it and the increased speed, Sargent decided to close the cab window on his side of the locomotive that was exposed to the elements. This was the second mistake Sargent made that night. The wind in his face had cooled the cab and was keeping him awake. Very soon after he closed the window, Engineer Sargent dozed off.

The sharp-eyed brakeman Oscar Timm, who had first spotted the hotbox in the middle of his train, was in the process of walking eastward from the caboose at the end of the circus train with a brightly lit fusee in one hand and a red-and-white lantern and emergency torpedoes in the other. At that point, the rear of the circus train caboose was 990 feet east of Ivanhoe Tower on the southern set of Michigan Central tracks. The switchover from the south to the north side of the dual-tracked Michigan Central was 925 feet east of Ivanhoe Tower.

The caboose Timm had just left was almost under the Ivanhoe Tower home signal bridge, and its wheels had not yet reached the G&W switch before halting. The last sleeping car immediately in front of the caboose was partially on the transition rails between the southern and northern Michigan Central tracks, and so was the third sleeper car directly ahead of it. The second and first sleepers were sitting on the north parallel track with the Hagenbeck-Wallace flatcars idle on the transition rails to the G&W trackage. Only the circus train locomotive, its tender and some of the wooden boxcars were fully on the G&W line.[53]

Suddenly, around the far east end of the curve, Timm saw the approaching smoke plume of Extra 8485 even before he could see the headlight of that oncoming train. By then, he had walked eastward along the railroad tracks about seven hundred feet from the rear of his own train. Timm took an instant to check that his emergency flares were burning brightly, lit another fusee and started to run toward the now-visible approaching headlight. Judging from the smoke exhaust coming from the troop train, he estimated the speed of that train to be about twenty-five miles per hour. Nothing yet indicated that his efforts were drawing any attention from the train's engineer, and he judged that he had time enough to jump over to the fireman's side of the track to try to alert that man to the danger.

Again, he was unsuccessful. Timm jumped back to the engineer's side of the locomotive, waving his arms and shouting in frustration as the steam engine swept by. As a last desperate measure, he even threw his burning fusee at the engineer's closed window. It hit the closed cab window with a small shower of sparks and bounced off. After that, all Timm could do was look on with horror as the rest of the troop train sped by.

Several members of the train crew on the Hagenbeck-Wallace Extra watched Brakeman Timm's failed actions. Engineer Gasper, looking backward from the circus train locomotive, saw Timm try to physically signal to the oncoming troop train and then saw him throw his lit fusee. Gasper initially assumed that the brakeman had successfully caught the engineer's attention and was simply discarding the device. Conductor R.W. Johnson also saw Timm's futile signaling effort; he was instantly horrified but was in no position to assist. He had grabbed the gear needed to fix the hotbox on the circus flatcar and was halfway between his caboose and the problem car when he first became aware of the approaching headlight on the track behind them. Brakeman Aust, up in the locomotive with Gasper and Fireman Phillips, also saw Timm attempt to stop 8485. When he didn't hear the engineer of that train blow the whistle in response to the signal, he jumped down from the locomotive cab and started running back toward the rear of his train.

Trainmaster Whipple, still inside the circus train caboose, probably had the best view of Timm's vain effort and must have been terrified to realize that the more than 150 tons of onrushing engine would not stop. He managed to jump or was thrown clear of the caboose's rear platform as the steel crumpled under the driven weight of a steam engine and its string of rail cars still moving under power at twenty-five miles per hour. The steel platform, steel frame, wheels and axles were instantly bent and twisted and were pushed forward into an unrecognizable mass that was then swept into a rolling pile caught on the grilled cowcatcher of Engine 8485. It and the engine behind it continued to drive forward and into the next car.

That next car was a sleeper with "Hagenbeck-Wallace number 5" painted on it; it was one of the circus's cars that had been converted into a two- or three-tiered bunk car for unmarried single men and women. The unrecognizable twisted mass of the caboose frame being pushed in front of Engine 8485's nose drove into and under the wood sleeper. In an instant, the engine began grinding and breaking everything in its path. Wall- and floorboards, frame timbers, bunks, fixtures, dividers, bedding and people were all added to that rolling mass of destruction. Some things and people were tossed aside, but most became part of the debris. After pushing its way completely through the rearmost sleeper, the engine impacted H&W sleeper number 16, treating it the same way and immediately adding it and its occupants to the pile being pushed by the engine's nose. Still, it continued on, smashing its way completely through sleeper 15 and most of the way through sleeper 17 before finally grinding to a halt.[54]

Engineer Gasper, still in the cab of Engine 7826 at the head of the circus train, later claimed that all he felt was a "slight shock," and then his air pump started working rapidly. Fireman Phillips, who was making his first-ever trip on that portion of the railroad division, was also in the cab of 7826 and independently backed up the engineer's description. Phillips said that just two minutes after his circus train stopped moving, he felt a shock much like one made during a routine coupling.

Conductor L. Johnson, at the time somewhere in the rear portion of the troop train, described his first indication of the collision as a shock that he attributed to a burst air hose and a continuous shove. Brakeman Jackson, riding in the caboose at the rear of troop train, later claimed that just before the collision he felt a jolt, something like the air brakes being applied in emergency mode. Then there was a second, less severe shock and then a third milder one. Still, the three successive jolts were hard enough to throw him over the seats and put out all his lights, even the marker lights. He also later admitted that he did not actually hear the sound of brakes being applied before the collision.[55]

For those bedded down in the circus train sleeping cars, the situation was totally different. Essentially, their cars were first split right down the middle and then turned to splintered rubbish around them—all the while they and the rest of the car's smashed contents were being shoveled forward. The most fortunate were actually thrown completely clear of the deadly trash pile, while a few others found themselves pushed toward the top of the pile. But there were many others who were encased in broken boards, bedding and beams, meshed in with iron wheels, carriage trucks and the now unbelievably grotesque shape of the steel caboose frame.

Without exception, the circus men, women and children in that tragedy never claimed to remember the sounds of the wreck, only the series of terrible scenes that followed immediately afterward. It was the people who crawled out of the wreckage who were the real "first responders" at the site. Henry Miller, an assistant light engineer for

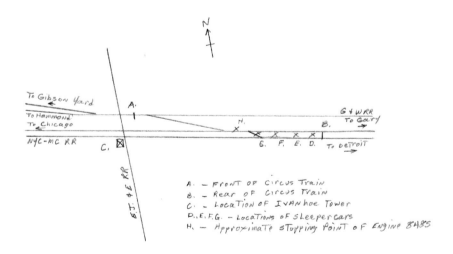

Diagram of the track pattern and approximate placement of the wrecked rail cars based on the official government investigation completed and filed in 1918.

the circus, was one of them. He was berthed in sleeper number 5, just ahead of the caboose, and he was one of the fortunate ones. His description, given later, was graphic:

> *I was in the last coach, next to the caboose. I woke up to the sound of splintering wood, and then, suddenly, I was sitting up. I thought it was a broken air line. Then there was another crash, and another, and another. I was pounded into the corner of my berth. My scalp was split open. The whole car buckled. It parted down the center as clean as though it had been sliced with a giant knife. I felt my section rising as the engine of the troop train ploughed into it. Then I was away up in the air on top of the wreckage in my shirt and drawers. I put down my head and lay still. A coat came sailing over and landed on top of me. Then everything was quiet. I started to climb down.*[56]

I.S. Steinhouser, an assistant property man, was berthed next to Miller in that last car. He later recalled:

> *I experienced a strained shoulder and back. My boss was killed. When I woke up, I thought someone had slugged me one in the neck. The engine passed through our car, and then went dead. I felt like I was under an apartment building. There was enough wood on me to build a ship. I clawed my way through it, and someone grabbed hold of me and jerked me out. I slid down into the ditch in my underwear and shivered. It was cold. I heard something and saw a pair of pants sailing through the air. I grabbed them. They were my pants!*[57]

It will never be known just how, or what, caused a fire to start in that pile of wreckage. Or what caused the several explosions that were heard once the wreckage began burning. Unnamed witnesses to the tragedy soon guessed that some overturned lighting equipment in the sleepers or possibly the locomotive firebox ignited the blaze. Investigators later discounted those guesses and focused on the oil lamps used in three of the sleepers. However, sleeper 17 had electrical lights, and the electrical system powering those lights did have a battery or capacitor of some sort. Perhaps a broken piece of metal caused an electrical short, or a loose electrical cable could have sparked and set the oil in those lamps on fire. No one could ever say exactly what caused the wreckage to burn. All did agree, however, that once the fire started, it spread quickly and burned deadly hot.

A.F. Roberts, the circus ticket seller, was in the last sleeper. He stated that the first thing he remembered were timbers falling around him, but since he did not become imprisoned, he was able to escape easily. Then he said, "I saw people burned alive in one great flaming hell of tortured souls and consumed flesh. God, the awfulness of it! And how brave were the injured who aided in rescues."[58]

There were only a few others berthed in sleeper number 5 who survived. One of the more fortunate was Joe Dierckx, who occupied a lower berth at the rear of the car nearest the caboose. His partner, Max Nietzborn, was asleep with him in this berth and was killed. Joe's brother, Arthur Dierckx, was mortally injured as well. Some individuals thought these three men were related since they did their act under the name Dierckx Brothers. As their publicity photo indicated, the Dierckx Brothers did a strongman act with elephants walking over a bridge held up in the center by the legs of the brothers, who were lying on their backs. Later, Nietzborn would be listed in the casualty report under the name Max Freehand, which he adopted when the United States declared war on Imperial Germany. The extent of anti-German sentiment immediately prior to the war had forced his name change.

One of the youngest rescuers was Bobbie Cottrell. Near the close of the 1890s, the Powell sisters, Louise and Margaret, toured Europe and thrilled many audiences with their riding act. During that tour, Margaret Powell met and married Robert Cottrell. Later, the three came to the United States and brought their act to the Hagenbeck-Wallace Circus. In 1899, Robert Jr. was born to the young couple, and during the 1917–18 academic year, young Bobbie attended school in Valparaiso, Indiana. He had joined his parents during the Michigan City engagement and was berthed with them in the same sleeper after the previous day's performance. As the troop train locomotive ploughed through their car, he was thrown upward through the displaced roof and landed outside, dazed but completely uninjured. By his heroic efforts, his parents were removed from the debris, also uninjured except for a few bruises. However, his aunt was across the aisle and had been killed instantly.

Bobbie was able to remove her limp body from the wreckage before the flames reached her.

Cottrell was not the only eighteen-year-old in that mess. Out of the wreckage, two teenagers—both boys who had run away to join the circus—appeared and began digging out others. They were Jimmie Mulvaney and J. Kurner from Steubenville, Ohio. Soon, a third youngster, James Everett from Memphis, Tennessee, joined them. All three had been with the circus since the beginning of the performance tour. Each was hampered by multiple cuts and bruises but was not seriously injured.

Henry Miller was one of the injured rescuers. Once he was safely clear of the debris and had his wits about him, he turned to doing what he could to help others:

> *I saw a hand waving, just a hand. It was turning in the air, grabbing for something. I got hold of it and started to pull. Then I saw there was a lot of paint cans on top of the man. I pulled and hauled and got them away. Then I saw that it was "Hickory," a wagon man. I kept jerking, and he kept hollering at me to let him alone. Right then, I saw the fire. It was creeping from the engine. Then the fire started to leap toward us. How I did work on that guy! I pulled him clear. Then we both rolled into the ravine. I got up when I got my breath. The fire was all over the wreck. It seemed that the cars were piled on top of each other. There were blood-chilling screams of men and women. I hung around and did what I could. One woman screamed, "God! O, God! Kill me! Kill me!"*[59]

Henry was not the only one who remembered that terrible cry; "Bud" Gorman, the equestrian director and circus horse master, heard it too. He returned to consciousness with a dead man lying on his chest. Beneath him, he could feel the jagged slivers of a broken board stabbing into his back. He managed to wriggle to freedom and quickly realized that flames were sweeping his way. Close by, he saw that some of the female survivors had spotted different men pinned under the debris and were hysterically trying to remove them. Assisted by clowns, now minus their makeup and costumes, the effort was failing, and the half-conscious victims, helpless under the crushing debris, were screaming: "Shoot me! Kill me! Don't let me be burned alive!"[60]

Mayme and Ed Ward were married in 1912 while on the road with the Ringling Brothers Circus. In 1914, they joined the Hagenbeck-Wallace Show, and by the early summer of 1918, they were the parents of two lively youngsters, one four years old and the other six months. Fortunately, the children were in the charge of Grandma Ward in Bloomington, Illinois. Mayme and Ed were in the lead sleeper, as befitted the stars of the Flying Wards, which also included Ed's sister, Jennie, and her husband, plus three others.

Mayme Ward later remembered that she was suddenly jolted back into an uncomprehending consciousness from a deep sleep. For one fleeting moment, she felt as if she were a contortionist. While she was on her back, her mattress had folded tightly and completely back; she was painfully aware that her feet were clear above her head, and she was in a rigid and immobile position. Almost stifled, she heard Alec W. Todd, her sister's husband, ask in a strangled tone, "You all right?"

She answered that she was and then said, "But I can't move."

Her brother-in-law pushed something, and she gradually was able to work her way out into the car's aisle. A moment later, he also wriggled free. The floor was a mess of jagged splinters, but Mayme and Alec did not notice it at the time. The roof of the car had slid down on their side, crushing the upper berth onto them.

Then Mayme heard a voice from above them saying, "Give me your hand. I'll pull you up." It was Charley Rooney, one of the bareback riders. As she went up, her long braided hair caught on projecting fragments of wood. "I didn't know you were so heavy," Rooney panted and then harshly jerked her up. Her hair parted company with her scalp, and she was suddenly up in the cool night air.

In the dim dawning light, she stared at chaos, utter chaos. What was a locomotive doing just opposite her, tilted slightly away and breathing out steam heavily? Why was she staring downward from a height above a telegraph pole? Theirs was the fourth car from the end, not counting the caboose. Where were the other cars? What was all this mass of steel and smoke—and what was that ominous red glow that was beginning to crackle like a wooden bonfire?

Alexander Todd pushed her roughly. "Get up that way," he gestured urgently, "and take care of yourself." He then disappeared into the smoke, steel and sudden flames, paying no heed to the glass that slashed savagely at his bare feet. He was looking for his wife, Jennie Ward Todd, in the berth opposite theirs. Shortly he found her and stumbled free of the debris with her limp, dead body in his arms. Gary's mayor William F. Hodges also remembered Alex Todd's reaction: "One man found the body of his wife in the weeds. He tried to comfort her. When he realized that she was dead, he just seemed to collapse. Rescuers shortly took him to the relief train."[61]

Mayme crawled away, vaguely noting that the wooden coaches, what was left of them, were "burning like a paper box." Fred Ledgett, the equestrian director, was now at her side. "I can't…breathe," he gasped hoarsely. Later he would learn that every one of his ribs was broken.

A numbing flash of pain struck Mayme, and she looked down at her feet. Every toe was dislocated; no two pointed in the same direction. She pointed out to Fred the weird condition of her toes in disbelief.

"Don't…make…me…laugh," he almost sobbed, and together they hobbled down the side of the track. Finally, they literally collapsed on a pile of ties, unaware that only a few tattered rags of their nightclothes remained to cover their bodies.[62]

Extra 7826's flagman, Timm, noticed Joe Dierckx: "I remember remarking to myself at the time that he had a beautiful physique. I did not have the faintest idea who he was." Both Joe and his brother Arthur, along with their partner Max, had been thrown clear of the wreckage. Max was already dead. Arthur was still breathing, but only Joe could get to his feet. Flagman Timm and others took Joe and his brother off to the side of the wreck, where Joe collapsed.[63]

In keeping with the tradition of circus society, general manager Charles Gollmar and his wife were in the fourth sleeper from the rear, occupying a stateroom as befitted their position. This sleeper had electric lights instead of the usual oil lamps and a few more amenities than the other Hagenbeck-Wallace sleepers in Extra 7826. It may have been slightly newer than the other cars as well.

Those extras did not help it survive any better, however. The roof was instantly torn from the car at the impact, and the engine of the troop train finally stopped immediately in front of the Gollmar stateroom. Neither Gollmar nor his wife was seriously injured, but an unidentified body was hurled into their room. Both of them got out of the car and tried to do what little they could.

At about the same time, or soon thereafter, Lon Moore, a circus clown, saw Mrs. Mary Enos, an air acrobat, trying to save her husband, Eugene. She had been thrust through a hole made in the side of the sleeper when the car started to buckle and break apart. She and Lon started to pull on Eugene's protruding hand. He was unconscious from the weight of debris that was crushing downward relentlessly. As if by a miracle, they were able to remove Eugene from the entanglement.

Later, after both she and her husband had been taken to the hospital, Mrs. Enos said, "God gave us strength to get him out before the flames licked him." Her husband was with her at the time she made that statement, and with short breaths between waves of piercing pain, he said, "Yes, I owe my life to her and Lon."[64]

At the age of fifty-two, Lon Moore was a survivor of the Hagenbeck-Wallace Circus train wreck at Durand, Michigan, in 1903. At that time, as well as on this date, he had been berthed in a sleeper occupied by Mr. Gollmar, the general manager.

The situation in sleeper 15, which was behind number 17, was worse. The berth next to the Wards was the vacated one that Stella Coyle and her children were using. It normally belonged to Anna Donovan, but Anna was not with the circus that night. Just a few seconds prior to the crash, Charley Rooney's sister met Mrs. Coyle taking one of the children to the washroom. Little Joe, asleep in his berth, was suddenly awakened and severely jolted to one side. A huge locomotive was moving up the aisle of the sleeper, accompanied by what seemed like the jarring of a great earthquake coupled with a deafening clap of thunder. He could not move, try as he might. About him was an unearthly glow. Eventually, he was able to move one hand. Then he heard the voice of his father.

Big Joe Coyle had been thrown clear of the wreckage with only minor injuries, and once he realized what had happened, he went looking for the other three members of his family. In response to his calls, Big Joe heard his son crying, "Oh, Papa, help me out of here!" In response, Big Joe started tearing madly at the burning timbers. The intense heat seared his hands. His great strength was of little help. Again, he heard, "Daddy! Help me out. I'm burning."

"Big Joe" Coyle, who lost his entire family in the tragedy. *Courtesy Miami County Museum.*

A great wave of flame suddenly swept over the debris, and several men had to pull Big Joe, dazed and badly burned, from the site. Much later, the remains of Little Joe would be found, and beneath Little Joe lay the fire-blackened bodies of Mrs. Coyle and the other child.[65]

It took a little time for the men in both train crews to get over the shock of the disaster and begin functioning again. Generally, the crewmen on the circus train appear to have reacted a little more quickly than the crew of 8485. After the collision, Engineer Gasper grabbed a fusee and ran ahead of his engine to flag down all eastbound traffic. Brakeman Aust went with him and, after helping to stop an eastbound freight, went back to his own train and uncoupled the connection between cars six and seven. In doing so, he discovered the reason there had not been much concussion felt in the cab of 7826. The first circus flatcar in his train had absorbed most of the impact and had broken in half, lifting the leading half of the broken car in the air, as well as the back end of the seventh of the freight cars on the string ahead of it. Fireman Phillips stayed on his engine and kept up steam pressure so that what was left of his train could be moved the moment the track was cleared.

Farther back on Extra 7826, Conductor R.W. Johnson was already running to Ivanhoe Tower to summon assistance when 8485 stopped. Once he was sure help had been called, he met Gasper to give him a short explanation for the unscheduled stop that had caused the accident. After that, he could only think of repairing the hotbox on flatcar 72, the task he was about to begin before the collision. Later, there was an unconfirmed story that he was heard talking to himself as he worked, saying, "I'm going to get fired for this!" over and over again.[66]

Flagman Timm was running back to his train as the collision occurred and passed Extra 8485's conductor, L. Johnson, without talking to him. He later said that he met 8485's fireman, Klaus, as that man climbed down from the third or fourth car in 8485's string. He said Klaus appeared dazed and unsteady on his feet. Timm said that he did not see Engineer Sargent at all and immediately got busy trying to rescue victims still trapped in the wreckage.

Conductor L. Johnson assisted Klaus from the roof of the car that he had been thrown onto and then crossed to the north side of the wreckage to help the rescue effort. There he saw Engineer Sargent and asked him what had happened. Sargent admitted that he had been asleep immediately prior to the collision. Both men began working independently with the rescue effort. Brakeman Jackson relit his rear markers and then came forward to assist with the rescue. On the way, he came upon Fireman Klaus, who was still dazed and stumbling toward the rear of 8485. Jackson asked Klaus how the accident had happened, and Klaus replied that the engineer was asleep.

Flagman Moyer seems to have been the most coherent crewman on 8485 at that moment. After the shock of the collision, he relit his lanterns and had Jackson do the same for the markers while he ran back eastward from the rear of his train to flag down the second train, which he knew was only a few minutes behind them. Once he had that second empty troop train halted, he uncoupled its engine from its consist string so that the engine could be used to pull back the sleeper cars of his own train and help clear the area around the wreck. He said that when he later looked back toward the site of the collision, he saw the whole sky lit up by the fire.

The wreckage pile pushed ahead of the troop train locomotive, which was still smoking when this photo was taken. *Courtesy Hammond Public Library.*

By that time, the porters from both empty troop trains were running forward with blankets and mattresses pulled out of empty berths. At the scene, they spread the bedding on the ground next to the tracks and helped the injured and dying achieve a small degree of comfort. Three of the troop train porters—Frank Clemons, L. Lewis and W. Dodson, generally known as the "Boys from Texas" or "the Texas trio"—also aided rescuing victims. Each burned his hands severely and later went to the hospital for treatment. Clemons recalled:

> *I didn't know what to do first. The first woman I came to kept screaming, "Don't touch me! Don't touch me!" The first man said, "Let me be. I'm dying!" We saw women burning alive. It was horrible…I never want to see a train wreck again.*[67]

Chapter 5

RESCUE AND REMEMBRANCE

The sonic boom of the crash vibrated glass windowpanes in houses near the tracks and brought local residents out into the predawn night to see what had caused the noise. The scene was evidently beyond immediate comprehension, and the onlookers froze at the edge of the wreck. Brakeman Oscar Timm noticed the first bystanders on the scene, gawking as if in a daze. "They were dumbfounded," he recalled in July 1968. "They were unable to move. I called to some to help and that seemed to jolt other people into action."[68]

Later, much later, the exact time of the accident would be fixed as occurring between 3:56 and 3:59 a.m., the darkest hour of June 22, and during the thirty minutes that followed, only the men from the trains, the surviving circus people and the nearby residents of the Ivanhoe district were available to deal with the disaster. But help was coming.

First to arrive was William Hodges, the newly elected mayor of Gary, Indiana, and that city's fire chief, Wilfred Grant. Both reached the scene in the fire chief's car about thirty minutes after the collision. What they beheld at first numbed their senses: shattered sleeping cars, twisted human forms partially seen beneath debris, crackling flames and the cries of helpless, desperate and despairing victims. All of that plus the smell of burning human flesh shook them badly. Still, they quickly became aware of the many injured and dazed persons taking shelter in

One of the local fire chiefs inspecting the wreckage after the fire was extinguished. *Courtesy Hammond Public Library.*

Railroad men inspect the wrecked New York Central locomotive 8485 amid onlookers. *Courtesy Hammond Public Library.*

the woods and dunes alongside the tracks. There was little they could do but help people move away from danger; however, their presence would become important as additional help arrived.

The first official rescuers to arrive were two fire companies dispatched from Hammond that reached the site soon after the mayor and Gary's fire chief. Seemingly only moments later, another contingent of firemen from Gary appeared. Chief Grant took charge of all three fire companies and began assigning tasks. Later, when Hammond's fire chief reached the scene, the two chiefs split the work, with each treating the side of the fire facing the direction of his respective city. That was not a bad decision as it allowed the fire to be approached from more than one direction.

Realizing that the huge fire consuming the wrecked rail cars could not be extinguished due to a lack of water, the chiefs initially directed the firemen to extricate those in the wreckage who could be safely reached. For the most part, the intense heat of the fire kept the firefighters from attacking the flames. Only in a few places were they able to remove a body after suppressing an edge of the fire with fire extinguishers and axes.

In the Gibson rail yard, only two or three miles to the west, special rescue trains and crews were being hastily marshaled. Still, precious minutes passed. Nearly an hour later, at 4:45 a.m., the first rescue train—after backing up to the site from the Gibson roundhouse about two miles west of the accident—arrived, and the water in its tender was made available to the firemen on the west side of the wreck.

During testimony given days later, the road foreman of engines for the Michigan Central/New York Central, who had been on the first section of the Hagenbeck-Wallace Circus train, reported that he had arrived in Hammond on that leading train at about 2:30 a.m. and was in the Hammond Switching Tower when the tower operators received the call from Ivanhoe Tower announcing the wreck. He was the one who had fixed the time that the first Gibson-based relief train reached the site. He also reported that some of the more physically able victims and other persons already there began rushing toward the incoming relief train cars for a variety of reasons.[69]

One of those on the rescue train was Mr. Nick Connelly, division superintendent for the Michigan Central, and thanks to his presence, some resemblance of order began to take shape. The rescuers began carrying the injured, unconscious or helpless several hundred feet to the rescue train. Then came the limp forms of those bodies that had been removed from the debris.

On the east side of the wreck, the second section of troop train 8485 had arrived at about the same time and was stopped behind the first train section. It also was quickly pressed into service as a rescue unit, and at six o'clock that morning, about one hour after arriving at the disaster and two hours after the wreck itself, it was ordered back to the crossing at South Broadway in Gary, where medical help was being assembled.

Other than being an observer, Mayor Hodges made his real contribution by organizing his city's medical response and acting as a magnet that drew the attention of newspaper reporters now showing up at the site. Telephone calls from the Ivanhoe Tower back to the Gary Tower alerted and summoned his city's medical facilities and people, and they assembled what was basically a triage center at a point where the patients could be transferred from the rail cars to ambulances. Mayor Hodges made available all of the ambulances in Gary, plus about fifty commandeered horse-drawn hacks and gasoline-powered automobiles. Doctors routed all those clad in Pullman blankets who were brought off the rail cars onto stretchers in preparation for the short trip to Gary's hospitals. Fractured skulls, broken bones and blood were common observations. All in all, it took about forty-five minutes to transfer the victims from the rescue train to shuttle conveyances and get them on the way to designated medical facilities.[70]

The evacuated victims went to four different hospitals in Gary and to St. Margaret's Hospital in Hammond. The majority of the injured circus people were taken eastward to Gary, but nearly as many uninjured survivors went to Hammond. The Michigan Central depot in Hammond became the western triage point where the injured were taken to St. Margaret's, while the uninjured joined their comrades who had reached that city on the first circus train.

Acrobats, trapeze performers and contortionists, the most athletically oriented of the circus staff, had forgotten their priceless legs at the accident site as they leaped into small holes in the wreckage to give aid to those pinned under debris, and at the hospitals, they continued

Beginning to clear the wreckage and debris with Ivanhoe Tower in the background. *Courtesy Hammond Public Library.*

Picking up one of the wheel trucks of the wrecked caboose that was on the rear of the circus train. *Courtesy Hammond Public Library.*

to help move the injured whenever necessary. Once in those hospitals, a whole new phase of the recovery effort was begun. Surviving cowpunchers from Wild West shows who had come to work for the Hagenbeck-Wallace Circus voluntarily acted as nurses. The hospital staff quickly found that they were quite adept at handling cuts, bruises and minor burns.

Hand in hand with the evacuation came the beginning of the removal and clearing phases of response. Concurrently with rescue operations on the east side of the wreck, as the second troop train took its load of survivors back eastward to Gary and thus opened the westbound track, a switch engine was dispatched with a crew and all equipment necessary to remove the Pullman cars that had been attached to the first troop train. Those twenty-one cars were pulled back to Gary and shunted onto empty sidings in various parts of that city's rail yard. Except for locomotive 8485 and its tender, jackknifed in a southwesterly direction across both the east- and westbound tracks, most of the westbound Michigan Central trackage was cleared. Only some of the still-blazing debris of the wooden cars was left.

At about that same time, another crew began clearance work on the west side of the wreck. One of the crewmen was Harry Van Valkenburg, who had been at home with his family at 49 Sibley Street in Hammond when he was pulled from his bed before daylight, probably sometime between 4:15 and 4:45 a.m., by a telephone call ordering him to report to the Michigan Central depot at the corner of Willow Court and Oakley Streets three blocks away. He would be a brakeman on the wrecking train crew that was being assembled to clear the west end of the blocked tracks.

When the wrecking crew arrived on scene, Jack Johnson, the wrecker boss, began giving orders. After making a quick assessment, Johnson realized that part of the second circus train ahead of the broken flatcar could easily be moved. The locomotive, tender and baggage cars at the head of that train were soon on their way to Hammond. That left the broken flatcar and the six others between it and the smoldering circus sleepers. The rearmost flatcar was still coupled to sleeper 17, and for the flatcars to be pulled clear, it had to be disconnected. Johnson told Harry Van Valkenburg and others to "pull that pin!"; this action was enough

A view of the rear of the troop train's tender and locomotive after the troop berthing cars were pulled away. *Courtesy Hammond Public Library.*

to separate those cars from the remains of the sleeper. After an easy tug by the repair-train engine, the rearmost flatcar settled into place on the rails. Moments later, the last undamaged portion of the circus train was pulled away.[71]

As the recovery effort progressed at the wreck site and the different right of ways were cleared, the surviving circus flatcars and their loaded wagons were brought to the performance ground in Hammond. All tents but the big top were erected, and several circus wagons were unloaded from the flatcars.

The Michigan Central westbound track was now entirely clear of equipment except for the jackknifed locomotive 8485 and the smoking embers of the wooden sleepers. The next thing to happen at the wreck site was moving the tender of the wrecking train locomotive as close to the fire as possible. With that tender in position, the water it contained became available to the firemen, and they were able to begin cooling the debris enough to resume searching for bodies. Once the flames were cooled sufficiently, a big hook on the steam-powered wrecking crane was swung over and reached out to began tearing apart the tangled steel and burning wood.

As trainmen were clearing the tracks of all remaining circus train equipment, rescuers were still probing the burning debris in search of dead or injured passengers. The recognizable body of Mrs. Mary

Cottrell was found, and at that point in time, she still had some of her valuable rings on her fingers. At another place, an axle and the attached two wheels of one of the demolished sleepers was found over the chest of a dead man. At that point, the heat was so intense that it was impossible to slip a chain over the axle so the big hook could lift the axle and wheels away.

Once fire hoses were put into action, the work progressed at a quicker pace, and the recovery of bodies from the wreckage commenced. The charred skull of a man was found beneath the cowcatcher of the tilted locomotive, and dismembered fingers lay along the track rails. One of the most ghastly sights was of two doomed men who could not be identified. They had been caught between two of the coaches, jammed together with mattresses all about them. The mattresses had caught fire, and the expressions of terror and pain were still visible on their blackened and charred faces, frozen in time.[72]

Estimates vary from one observer to another, but it was becoming abundantly clear to both rescuers and spectators that the locomotive had plowed through the sleeping cars some four to five hundred feet before coming to a complete stop. When New York Central 8485 was lifted and put back on the tracks, the surprising discovery was that not one person had been crushed under the engine. As it drove through the caboose and sleeper numbers 5, 15 and 16, locomotive 8485 had literally rolled up all

The crowd of spectators that gathered at the wreck as the cleanup and recovery began. *Courtesy Hammond Public Library.*

The steel berthing cars, borrowed from the Canadian Pacific Railroad, that made up the troop train called Extra 8485 and jumped tracks during the collision. *Courtesy Hammond Public Library.*

Clearing wreckage with Ivanhoe Tower at the far right. *Courtesy Hammond Public Library.*

of the broken parts of those different cars, as well as quite a few bodies, into a pile that was actually shoved under Mr. Gollmar's car, sleeper 17. Except for the few who were tossed clear or pulled from the rubble, those trapped in that rolling pile never had a chance.

Two cranes place one of the troop train cars back on its tracks. *Courtesy Hammond Public Library*.

The front end of locomotive 8485 prior to being righted and put back on the tracks. The passenger car on the right is from one of the rescue trains that came from Gibson rail yard. Ivanhoe Tower, at the far side of the passenger car, can not be see, but the shifting rods connecting the tower to the rail switches are visible. *Courtesy Hammond Public Library*.

Morticians were standing by to quickly remove the bodies as continuous water from locomotive tenders suppressed the flames. Once the pile was sufficiently cooled to allow removal of the dead, the remains were loaded onto the morticians' wagons and taken to the various funeral parlors throughout Gary and Hammond.

The evening newspaper initially carried reports of eight dead in the Gary morgue and had a bulletin inserted that another twelve had been added to that count. In another part of that same newspaper, a page gave the estimates of about forty dead, another thirty injured who were expected to die and about eighty more injured with a good chance of survival. Apparently, half of the estimated dead were taken to Hammond and half to Gary. Already, two men and one woman had expired after reaching Hammond. One of them was Arthur Dierckx. More would soon join them.[73]

Evidently, there was enough confusion over the rescue work to baffle a newspaper reporter who was trying to sort out the facts of the effort. In the newspaper edition put out that evening, he criticized one Hammond undertaker for loading a body onto his hearse instead of an injured woman who needed to go to the hospital.

Undertaker E.J. Burns first explained that he had been called by Hammond police at 4:30 a.m. and asked if his ambulance was available.

The horse-drawn ambulance operated by the Emmerling Funeral Home in front of St. Margaret Hospital in 1917. This ambulance was one of many used to transport wreck victims. *Courtesy Hammond Public Library.*

Responding that his ambulance was in Chicago, Burns's conversation with the police ended, and he went back to sleep. At about 8:00 a.m., the police called him again and told him to get out to the crash site with his hearse. Once there, he loaded several charred bodies onto his hearse and brought them back to his mortuary in Hammond. Soon thereafter, he got another call from the Hammond police instructing him to go to the Michigan Central depot and recover another body that had been brought there. That's when the newspaper reporter saw the behavior he did not understand. As Undertaker Burns later explained:

> *I intended to take the wounded woman but I saw the other ambulance* [there] *and thought it was there to take the woman. The corpse was in front of* [the door and] *the woman and to get her we would have had to go over the corpse, which I started to do, but the other ambulance man said, "You take the corpse and I'll take the wounded."* [74]

The newspaper printed the above episode as a means of apologizing for the harsh statements of the reporter in the previous edition. Still, the reporter's initial criticism illustrated the local reaction of remorse and regret that swept the communities. Overall, about twenty or so people were taken to the hospital in Hammond, while over one hundred went to the hospitals in Gary.

Mayme Ward was taken to Hammond's St. Margaret's Hospital along with the Dierckx brothers. There, Mayme's broken toes were treated, and she spent several weeks in the hospital's wards helping other circus members recover. Among them were three other members of the Ward trapeze act. Once they were released from the hospital, what was left of the Flying Wards returned to their home in Bloomington, Illinois, and sat out the rest of the year.

Thirty-five-year-old Joe Dierckx was also one of those victims admitted to St. Margaret's Hospital. He remained unconscious for thirty hours after he was admitted. When he awoke, the first thing he saw was a nurse, Miss Marie Jones, who was the sister of Mrs. Knute Rockne, wife of the late Notre Dame football coach. Joe had a skull fracture and multiple fractures of the jaw and one of his legs, as well as temporary paralysis on one side of his body. It was not surprising that those injuries kept him in the hospital longer than most other victims. About four months and three operations later, Nurse Jones became Mrs. Joseph Dierckx, and soon thereafter, the couple moved to Maryland, where Joe continued recuperating from his injuries. Unfortunately, he never regained his former agility and was forced to find another calling. In 1921, he and his wife returned to Indiana, moving to South Bend at Mrs. Rockne's request, and in 1930, Joe became head custodian at Notre Dame stadium.[75]

Over in Gary, 104 injured were being treated at four different hospitals. One of those was Jennie Ward Todd of the Flying Wards, who, along with her husband, Alexander Todd, had initially been taken to Mercy Hospital. She was pronounced dead on arrival and sent to the city morgue, while her husband was admitted temporarily for observation. Most of the other twenty-eight circus people who were also treated at Mercy Hospital were released that same day. The admittance record for Mercy Hospital that day revealed that most of the circus patients admitted were diagnosed with bruises, but some of them were suffering from severe trauma-type injuries like fractured or broken bones. One performer, the only one listed as being Jewish, had a broken neck and died eleven days later. Another ten were kept in the hospital for anywhere between one and eighteen days. One other fact gleaned from that hospital record was that six of those circus people treated at Mercy Hospital were listed as "Negro," and one of them was kept overnight for observation.[76]

By midmorning, news of the Hagenbeck-Wallace Circus train disaster had spread throughout most of Hammond and Gary. The anticipating patrons of the circus who had not yet heard the news were informed as they gathered along the proposed circus parade route. Most of the younger children and women stayed away from the ghastly activities centered on the Michigan Central depot and the tracks leading to the wreck site. Others traveled out to the scene of disaster. Many rode to the area on the Hammond–Gary interurban cars. Others came by automobile, and photographs taken at the wreck showed that some even rode bicycles to the scene.

At that point, rescue and recovery operations were still underway, and when the curious arrived, they gazed with morbid fascination at the work going on. There were still some unforgettable scenes to see. The evacuation of the injured and dying was soon over, but some of the uninjured were

The first train to pass the scene of the wreck. It was another troop transport loaded with soldiers bound for France. *Courtesy Hammond Public Library.*

still on the scene and were themselves objects of curiosity. There was also the twisted steel and smoking wood and, in many cases, the black charred remains of human forms. A growing number of sheriff's deputies and firemen, supplemented by railway detectives, feebly attempted to keep the onlookers away from the operations area, but photographers' pictures amply show how unsuccessful that effort was. The pictures also show the first train to pass the site once the rails were cleared and pronounced fit for use. It was full of troops, some of whom were still standing out on the vestibules of their cars and staring at the remains of the wreck that had delayed their journey to war.

As so often happens, as the crowd grew in size, it attracted a percentage of the criminal element. From the many complaints received by officers of the law, it was later apparent that pickpockets were doing a flourishing business in the midst of the huge humanitarian effort. The number of theft victims, the number and value of items stolen and the number of shysters caught were never reported.

The Hagenbeck-Wallace ticket wagon that was used by Manager Gollmar when he was preparing the casualty list. *Courtesy Miami County Museum.*

Among the curious in that crowd was a nineteen-year-old DePauw University student of journalism who was working that summer as a cub reporter for one of the Gary papers. He had come out to the crash in search of a human interest story. At first, he walked gingerly along the side of the track—a recent pathway now strewn with debris—and observed the rescue and evacuation activity. Then he collared Mayor Hodges, who summarized the situation:

> *It was one of the worst wrecks I have ever witnessed. The injured were lying in many different places. Bodies of the dead were strewn along the tracks. The cars were in flames. We saw several bodies in the ruins. Someone said that there were twenty-five bodies in the remains of one car. Most of these were women.*[77]

Later a pathos-ridden tale appeared in a leading Chicago journal. The facts had been culled directly from the cub reporter's material, which had been published previously in the *Gary Tribune.* No one in that crowd could have ever dreamed that David E. Lilienthal, the cub reporter, would become the first chairman of the United States Atomic Energy Commission.

Chapter 6

GILDED MISERY

S ometime that morning, Ed Ballard, owner of the Hagenbeck-Wallace Circus, received a hurried telephone call from his secretary, Mr. Harry Sarig, who had traveled into Hammond on the first circus train. When told of the wreck, Ballard immediately arranged for an automobile to drive him from Chicago's Congress Hotel, where he had spent the previous night, and deliver him to Hammond as fast as possible.[78] When he finally reached the circus show grounds in Hammond, Ballard took charge and began restoring order to his shocked circus family. Ed Ballard was just the sort of man to do that.

Charles Edward Ballard was the third son of James "Big Jim" Ballard, who was born in the family log cabin in Orange County, Indiana, in 1874. He was a second-generation native of Orange County and came from a typical Hoosier farm heritage, a background that translated into the characteristics of being long in terms of determination, charity and hard work and short in terms of cash, influence and education.

In an odd way, it was probably his mother, Mary Elizabeth Ballard, who had the most influence on the direction her third son would take. She was perhaps the hardest-working member of her family and ingrained her work ethic into her children by example. A strict woman with strong religious beliefs, she took in laundry from the hotel and its guests in the area. It was not surprising, then, when her third son's first job was at one of the nicest hotels in the area as a pinsetter in the hotel's bowling alley.[79]

She would not allow a deck of cards in her home, and she most likely did not tolerate the use of alcohol, either, so the next turn of events in Ed Ballard's life was in direct contrast to that custom. Sometime toward the end of 1893, when Ed was nineteen and working as a rural mail carrier, he decided that his life's work would require renouncing his mother's values and investigating the opportunities that her inclination forbid. Consequently, he quit his job, took another as a bartender in a saloon in Paoli, Indiana, and began running his own small-stakes poker game in one of the saloon's back rooms. Of course, another rumor persists that instead of being a bartender, he was first employed as a swamper (janitor) who cleaned, among other things, the spittoons in the place.

Regardless of what job he had in that Paoli saloon, he soon realized that the limited success of his own gambling enterprise was due to the location. Consequently, a year later, he departed the small country town and relocated back to West Baden, Indiana, where he managed the gambling operations of the Dead Rat Saloon. By the end of 1894, Ed owned the Dead Rat Saloon, and his success was soon brought to the attention of the owner of the West Baden Springs Hotel, the palatial health resort and spa being touted as "the Carlsbad of America." It was the same place where Ed had once worked as a bowling-alley pinsetter.

Offered quietly by the hotel as a "gentleman's entertainment" due to the limitations imposed by the hotel owner's wife, a highly profitable casino was already operating within the hotel, but its manager was not living up to expectations. Twenty-one-year-old Ed Ballard was offered the job, and he quickly accepted.

Ten years later, Ed Ballard was a young millionaire with interests in casinos at the hot springs in West Baden and French Lick in Indiana, Mackinac Island in Michigan, Miami Beach in Florida and Saratoga in New York. He also had his own hotel opposite the street entrance of the West Baden Springs Resort, plus a variety of other farm properties throughout southwestern Indiana. He finally married in 1913 and soon began building a beautiful brick mansion located in a central, prominent location on the avenue separating West Baden and the village of French Lick. His home still stands as evidence of his reputation for quality and style.[80]

The work that Ballard did once he got to Hammond and joined the gathering of circus performers, roustabouts and staff was proudly described in the July 6, 1918 edition of *Billboard Magazine*. Using the words "manliness and big-heartedness," the article told of how Ballard went about verifying the presence or absence of individuals, checked on their condition, visited those in hospitals and immediately paid for new clothing for all those who had lost nearly everything. Ballard also had lots of help from the citizens and merchants of Hammond, who began offering whatever assistance was needed even before they were asked.

Mr. Edward P. Neuman, the president of the U.S. Tent and Awning Company of Chicago, the company scheduled to deliver the new big-top tent in Hammond that day, was soon to become a key figure in the recovery effort. He appeared that afternoon with the new tent and a full crew of handlers, and they soon went to work. With so many of the Hagenbeck-Wallace canvas handlers either dead or injured, that extra assistance was vital in getting the old big-top canvas off the specially built spool wagons and the new canvas respooled into place. How many from that crew agreed to accompany the circus on to its next play date is not known. What is known is that Mr. Neuman became a major source of assistance in the funeral arrangements that were yet to follow.

Another key figure to win the praise of all who were there was General Manager Gollmar. He had already won the gratitude of all circus employees by rescuing the strongbox, which had been secured in his sleeping compartment. The wood and metal box had visible signs of the fire's intense heat, and the rings, bracelets and other valuables it contained were distorted beyond usefulness, but at least it had not been stolen once it was pulled from the flames.

Now Gollmar began the sad duty of determining who was still alive, what condition they were in and where they were. For that purpose, the ticket wagon was moved over by the cook tent, and Gollmar sat himself inside it with the circus payroll in hand. One by one, those who were present filed by. Gollmar then did two things: he verified their presence and condition and asked them if they wanted to remain with the show. Later that evening, Gollmar issued a statement declaring that two hundred of the six hundred Hagenbeck-Wallace employees were missing. Most of them, he thought, were canvas handlers and drivers, and only a small percentage

Winter quarters in
Peru, Indiana. *Courtesy
Miami County Museum.*

was performing artists. That figure of two hundred missing included both
the unidentified dead and those taken to the several area hospitals.[81]

Word of the Hagenbeck-Wallace disaster was already spreading across the
country by the time. Both the Ringling Brothers and Barnum & Bailey shows,
two different organizations in those days, sent telegraph messages offering
the Hagenbeck-Wallace Circus whatever assistance was needed in the way of
animals, equipment or performers to put the show back on the road.

That would not happen immediately, but it did happen a couple of
days later. Obviously, and to the ever-lasting disappointment of five-year-
old Warren A. Reeder Jr., the Hammond performance did not happen.
It is now doubtful that anyone other than that disappointed five-year-old
even thought about missing the show. A few less seriously injured circus
staff who were listed among the missing were released from the hospitals
and rejoined their friends and relatives on the show grounds that evening.

The next day was a Sunday, and true to form, Ballard and Gollmar
kept to the show schedule by staying in Hammond. That let seventeen-
year-old Jennie Maystack, an African American girl from Montgomery,
Alabama, who had suffered a dislocated shoulder in the wreck and spent
the night in Gary's Mercy Hospital, rejoin the show. In hopes that more
injured employees could soon rejoin, the circus held over in Hammond
until Monday morning before moving on. It had been scheduled to play
in Monroe, Wisconsin, but skipped that location in favor of the extra
time it gave the show to reorganize and restructure.[82]

On June 25, the show did indeed go on. The *Hammond Times* newspaper
dated June 26, 1918, ran the following front-page article:

BELOIT, WIS., June 25.—Like the Phoenix of fable, the Hagenbeck-Wallace circus emerged from its baptism of death and fire into the limelight here tonight with all the tinsel and glare so dear to devotees of "the big-top." Except for what they read in the newspapers, the general public was unable to tell that the big amusement enterprise had all but been wiped out…The music, the calliope, the bright lights, the clowns, the beautiful equestriennes, and the trapeze performers were all there and the performance took place with characteristic "snap and pep."[83]

But that was only part of the story—in fact, just the first two paragraphs of it. It went on to tell of the overshadowing sad memories that could be vaguely recognized by adults and even by some of the young. It seemed that the infectious gaiety, the spontaneity and the happy-go-lucky attitude of previous days was gone.

If a person were on scene to watch the Hagenbeck-Wallace Circus's arrival in Beloit and its set-up activity preparing for that performance, evidence of the Ivanhoe wreck would have been easy to see. A large number of the workers were wearing bandages. Many of the injured, who had been so recently discharged from the hospitals of Gary and Hammond, were too exhausted, sore and crippled to do more than watch the tents and equipment being put into place.

What the crowd could not see—was not allowed to see—was the heartbreak hidden by greasepaint and rouge. Of the twenty-five acts in the show on June 21, all but one of them had been affected by the Ivanhoe wreck tragedy. The Flying Wards and the McDu Sisters were not the trapeze artists in that performance; their acts were replaced by one borrowed from another circus that appeared in the show for the first time that evening. The Cottrell equestrians were performing that night, but one member of the act had died in the accident of June 22 and had since been replaced by a capable stranger sent by another show. When the band began the tune cuing that stranger to perform a solo portion of the act, Ed Cottrell fled the arena to cry in the dressing room.

Sometime that evening, a local reporter asked a Hagenbeck-Wallace veteran, one of the animal trainers, how many of the circus animals had survived the wreck. The answer was given in a soft monotone that could not hide the man's sense of inner anguish:

No, Mam, not an animal was killed. They were all in the first section ahead of the next section. Only people was killed. This place ain't the same. We all ain't here. The actors can't get their minds to working straight. It's all so-so… The lady that trains that lion over there was burned to death. Her partner ain't half doing his act. I know. He just naturally can't.[84]

The male performer that trainer described was Ben Hecht, who had survived the tragedy. His deceased partner was Millie Jewell from Washington, D.C.; she would be buried the next day.

Lon Moore, one of the many clowns who cavorted in front of the audience with exaggerated slapstick humor throughout the performance, broke down in tears when he returned to the dressing room. He alternated between calling out the names of his friends Eddie Devoe and George Donahue (who had died amid the burning timbers and would also be buried the following day) with the name of Emil Schwyer, the man who had pulled Moore from the wreck. In the days to come, Moore would follow Schwyer around the circus, repeatedly thanking him for the deed.

There had been more than one hero on June 22, and while Lon Moore's behavior and gratitude toward his hero were more than a little alarming, there was widespread recognition of the deeds of others. For instance, "Blackie" James Logan, a wagon driver, had dug his way into the wreckage of the accident and rescued the wife of the show's trainmaster when all hope had been abandoned of getting her out alive. Then there was Bill Curtis, who stayed and worked with other rescuers and firefighters until the last body was recovered. Both were back on the job but feeling the effects of the tragedy psychologically if not physically.

Anna Donovan, one of the wardrobe mistresses, aptly described the feeling beneath the tinsel, paint and gilded glamour of the traveling circus when she said:

And yet, we have to go on. It is business. It is our bread and butter. We have homes to maintain and families to support and bring up. We have to make them become educated and useful citizens. We are honest and pay our bills. We have respect for the law. We could not stop to mourn and put on black. We had to go on, no matter how we did feel inside.[85]

Chapter 7

CLOSURE

While the Hagenbeck-Wallace show was preparing for its performance in Beloit, Wisconsin, a coroner's inquest was convening at the Lake County Superior Court courthouse in Hammond, just two or three blocks north of St. Margaret's Hospital. The death of strongman Arthur Dierckx was cited as the main reason for the inquest, but everyone knew that his name was merely one of several that could have been used to summon the hearing. Lake County deputy coroner H.C. Green was the man actually conducting the inquest, and he summoned a host of witnesses who would later appear in many of the following investigations and trials held in various different parts of the Midwest during the next seven years.

Doctor B.W. Chidlaw was one of the first to testify regarding the handwritten deposition he had submitted on Arthur Dierckx's medical condition upon Dierckx's admittance to the hospital. Misters E.J. Burns and Nicholas Emmerling were also called to testify. Both were Hammond undertakers who had operated ambulances used in transporting the dead and injured from the Michigan Central depot to the hospital and morgue.

Then the inquest turned to determining the causes for Dierckx's condition and began hearing testimony from the train crew of Extra 8485: Edward F. Burgess, fireman on that train from Jackson, Michigan, to Michigan City, Indiana; brakemen W.R. Jackson and James Moyer,

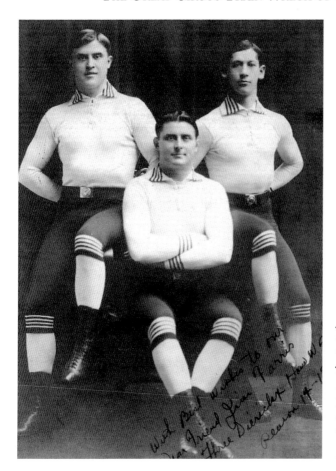

Joe Dierckx (left), Arthur Dierckx (center) and Max Nietzborn. Joe was the only one of the trio to recover from the accident. Max was killed during the wreck, and his brother, Arthur, died within a few days. *Courtesy Circus Hall of Fame.*

both of whom were on the train for entire run; and conductor Lewis Johnson, also on that train for the entire run. Next came testimony from the train crew for the Hagenbeck-Wallace train, especially brakeman Oscar Timm and conductor R.W. Johnson.

Railroad lawyers from the Michigan Central would not let either Alonzo Sargent, engineer for Extra 8485, or fireman Gustave Klauss, who went aboard that engine at Michigan City, testify at the inquest. However, Deputy Coroner Green did not need the engineer's and fireman's statements; enough information was gathered from the other witnesses for the coroner to return a verdict of "carelessness and negligence of the Michigan Central Railroad by reason of the carelessness of its employees, namely, the engineer and fireman on engine 8485 on June 22, 1918."[86]

Hand in glove with the inquest, on June 25, 1918, came the first lawsuit involving an injury to a Hagenbeck-Wallace performer, George A. Donahue, a clown who was confined to St. Margaret's Hospital with a broken back. During the next three years, there would be many more Unfortunately, George Donahue did not live long enough to reap any benefit from the legal action begun in his name. By September 24, 1924, when the last of the cases was finalized and dismissed, a total of 125 lawsuits had been filed that sought monetary relief for wreck victims exceeding $1,000,000. All of those lawsuits were influenced by numerous events.

The coroner's jury verdict was further reinforced by findings from the state and federal governments. At the time of the coroner's inquest, the Bureau of Safety within the Interstate Commerce Commission, in conjunction with the Indiana Public Service Commission, had already announced that a joint investigation regarding the accident would be held. The report of that investigation, as completed and filed on August 8, 1918, clearly ruled out any failure of the automated track signals, any failure of the brake system in place on Extra 8485 or any tower operator fault. It also ruled out any liability of the federal government for allowing the operation of wooden cars on the nation's rail system. It placed the blame for the accident squarely on Engineer Sargent for falling asleep and blame for the high number of casualties on the Hagenbeck-Wallace Circus for operating wooden cars instead of steel ones.

By that time, and based solely on the findings of the coroner's inquest, criminal charges were soon filed against both Engineer Sargent and Fireman Klauss, and the men were ordered to be held without bail for trial. That trial, the *State of Indiana v. Alonzo Sargent*, began in the Lake County Criminal Courtroom of the Lake County Courthouse in Crown Point, Indiana, on April 15, 1919, with Judge Martin Smith presiding. Lake County deputy prosecutor W.O. Thomas acted as representative for the state, and attorneys William J. McAleer and John A. Gavit, both from Hammond, represented Sargent and Klauss. Following a full day of testimony, pulled out from many of the same witnesses who appeared at the coroner's inquest, the jury was sent to deliberations, which lasted only four or five hours. Having determined that they were hopelessly deadlocked, they reported back to Judge Smith that they could not reach a verdict, and the judge declared the entire affair a mistrial. The Lake County prosecutor, Clyde Hunter, declined to retry the case, and it was dismissed in total on June 9, nearly a year after the accident.

In the other trials that followed over the next five years, much of the same resulted, and the Michigan Central Railroad, which many believed was the real culprit behind the accident, was basically absolved of all responsibility for contributing to it. Engineer Alonzo Sargent certainly was not absolved, however. Essentially, his thirty-plus-year career with the Michigan Central Railroad was over. Remaining in Jackson, Michigan, for the rest of his life, Sargent died at the age of seventy-five on May 7, 1942, still mindful of the terrible accident that killed 86 men, women and children and injured another 127 people.[87]

On June 26, 1918, the day following the first traumatic circus performance in Beloit and the inquest held in Hammond, a large funeral service was held for a majority of the Hagenbeck-Wallace dead. It was held at Woodlawn Cemetery in the Forest Park section of Chicago, where the Showmen's League, a guild for entertainers and performers founded by William F. "Buffalo Bill" Cody and now under the direction of league president John B. Warren, owned a good-sized plot of land purchased earlier that same year. At the time, Mr. Warren was lying on his own deathbed; still, despite his doctor's advice, he insisted on directing all necessary arrangements. The man actually footing the bill for the funeral service was Ed Ballard.

In a large common grave measuring thirty-five feet long by twenty-four feet wide dug down to five feet below the surface, the caskets of fifty-six victims of the Hagenbeck-Wallace tragedy were laid to rest. Warren himself died only a few days later, although it is not known if he, too, was interred in that plot. Also unknown were the names of most of the people who were placed in that mass grave. Only thirteen of the fifty-six bodies had been identified, which meant that the other forty-three bodies had been burned beyond recognition. Among those identified and buried there were Arthur Dierckx, Jeanette Roderick Barnett and her sister, Mary Roderick (commonly billed as the McDu Sisters), and the three members of "Big" Joe Coyle's family who died in the wreck.

Known or not, the graveside service officiated by Reverend Colonel F.J. Owens, chaplain of the Showmen's League; Reverend Johnston

Meyers from the Immanuel Baptist Church; and Father William Cahill from St. Mary's Roman Catholic Church in Riverside, Illinois, drew a crowd of over fifteen hundred friends, relatives and mourners, with "Big Joe" Coyle the most prominent. Also prominent was the large floral display sent by George M. Cohan, the famous stage actor and producer. That flower arrangement, and the thousands of other floral tributes surrounding the grave and its crowd of mourners, stood watch over the mass grave once the service was concluded and the crowd, including a devastated Joe Coyle accompanied by his relatives, walked away.

One person who was not present that day was the owner of the Hagenbeck-Wallace Show. He was back on the road, traveling with the partially reorganized show from Beloit, Wisconsin, to the next stop on the circus tour. A successful finish for the entire season's route was essential. But the conclusion of the 1918 performance tour on Chicago's Lake Michigan shore on September 29 would mark the last time Ed Ballard ever traveled with the Hagenbeck-Wallace Circus.[88]

Essentially, the 1918 performance season had not been all that much of a financial success even before the tragedy at Ivanhoe Tower. In previous years, the circus had traveled in a total of fifty-seven rail cars, but due to wartime restrictions, a shortage of help and the personnel disruption resulting from the military draft, the show had started out in just forty-nine rail cars. The mood of the nation and its concentration on the military buildup and armaments production tended to keep people focused on the affairs in Europe and away from less dramatic entertainments. In addition, the season had been an unusually wet one, dampening enthusiasm and all-too-frequently persuading potential circus-goers to stay at home. All of those factors on top of the accident, plus the $300,000 that Ed Ballard reportedly spent paying all claims resulting from the wreck, put the Hagenbeck-Wallace Circus Operating Company into bankruptcy and, once it returned to its winter quarters that fall, into receivership.[89]

On December 28 of that year, the show's operating company was sold to the partnership of a Mr. Jerry Mugivan and Mr. Bert Bowers for the bargain-basement price of $36,100. Ed Ballard was eligible to bid on the show but declined to do so at that time. So what did Mugivan and Bowers get for their money? According to the January 4, 1919 edition of *Billboard Magazine*, the partnership got

[the] *good will and trade name and property which included twenty-five flatcars, twelve stock cars, two advertising cars, one store car, eight sleeping coaches* [evidently, the wrecked four sleepers were immediately replaced by others], *one private coach, horses, ponies, ten elephants, six camels, five hybrid zebras, six lions, buffalo, two ostriches, six monkeys; thirty-six parade wagons including twenty-one wild animal cages; fifty-five baggage wagons, three canvas spool wagons, two pole wagons, two stake drivers, two dynamic lighting plants, one complete gasoline lighting system, two 45 horse-power Knox tractors, one patented gasoline cooking system, one complete set of blocks, poles, and seats, and harness for 220 head of horses.*

Actually, it was only the operating company that was bankrupt. The American Circus Corporation and Ed Ballard personally were financially sound, despite the disastrous year. Ballard just had other priorities right then and needed to turn his attention in another direction. With a new baby at home (his firstborn) and with some aspects of the deal to purchase the palatial West Baden Springs Hotel, the place where he had secured his first job, still being worked out, it was not surprising that he did not participate in the sale. However, he had not lost interest in performing circuses. Only a few months later, he and a new set of partners would again own the Hagenbeck-Wallace Circus. They would then purchase three more traveling shows for the American Circus Corporation.

In 1919, after spending the winter in the French Lick/West Baden area of southern Indiana, the Hagenbeck-Wallace Circus again went forth on the road, this time under the management of partner Bert Bowers. One of the positive things that Bowers did was to cut the show down to only thirty rail cars, an act that returned its season tours to highly profitable ventures. The show closed that year in Jackson, Tennessee, and then returned to West Baden, Indiana, for the winter. The 1920 tour saw the Hagenbeck-Wallace hitting the railways in new seventy- and seventy-two-foot steel rail cars. It would be quite some time before the other three circuses owned by the corporation also got rid of their wooden rail equipment, but never again would the Hagenbeck-Wallace Circus be involved in a deadly railroad accident. Once again, the show returned to spend the winter months of 1920–21 in southern Indiana, while the corporation's John Robinson Circus stayed at Peru's winter quarters in the middle of the state.

Old Ben Wallace, the man who had started the Hagenbeck-Wallace traveling show thirty-five years earlier, died in Peru, Indiana, in early April 1921, and the following October, his estate, including the winter quarters on the even older Miami Indian Reservation, was purchased by the American Circus Corporation. The price reportedly paid for the property, miscellaneous equipment, the yards, the workshops and the circus railroad cars owned by Wallace totaled $500,000. Since Jerry Mugivan was in the process of retiring from active management in the corporation and Bert Bowers was actively managing the status of four separate circuses, that corporate move was strictly Ed Ballard's choice. It was a good one, and it allowed the Hagenbeck-Wallace and the John Robinson shows to swap winter-quarter locations in 1923. They kept those arrangements throughout the remaining life of the corporation.

During the 1920s, traveling circuses were a robust life. Changes in management personnel, performers and tour routines marked what some have called the Golden Age of circuses, and this certainly was evident in the American Circus Corporation. The Flying Wards once again graced the upper reaches of the big top; an eighteen-year-old youngster named Clyde Beatty got his first job in one of the corporation's circuses cleaning out animal cages; clown Emmitt Kelly, who was in another show, met another performer who became his wife; and a youngster with the last name of Skelton, whose father was also a clown, grew into adulthood and stardom as "Red" Skelton. In the decades yet to come, those performers would become famous and nationally known celebrities of movies and television. Also during that period, they would be joined by an already famous Hollywood movie star named Tom Mix, who was an instant major attraction to another one of the corporation's shows that wintered in Peru, Indiana.

With five circuses going out on tour in the springs of 1928 and 1929, the American Circus Corporation really was at the top of the entire circus world. Only John Ringling, the surviving brother of the famous Ringling Brothers, could be considered true competition. But since the Ringling shows could only muster 90 rail cars in contrast to the 145 cars it took to transport Ballard's shows, the competition was not that close.[90]

Spectators watching the recovery work. *Courtesy Hammond Public Library.*

However, after bringing Tom Mix into the equation and out-foxing John Ringling over a four-week contract that brought the Hagenbeck-Wallace to Madison Square Gardens, Ballard received a message from John Ringling, in effect demanding that one of them buy out the other and end the battle. Consequently, just six short weeks before the crash of Wall Street on October 29, 1929, the American Circus Corporation was sold to the Ringling Brothers Corporation and ceased to exist.

But the Hagenbeck-Wallace Circus did not disappear—yet. Owned by Ringling, it continued operating until 1936. It was not the only fatality that year. John Ringling, Bert Bowers and Ed Ballard also died in 1936, and with their passing, the Golden Age of circuses died, too.[91]

CONCLUSION

T he death of the Golden Age of circuses was not, however, the death of the traveling tent circus. They continued to take to the rails every spring, departing from their home bases in northern and southern Indiana, only to return in the late summer and early fall. The tent shows were reduced to about thirty or forty rail cars, but the reduced number was offset by an increased size and weight capacity for each car. The wooden rail cars were long gone by then, so the speed and safety of the circus trains was vastly improved.

The acts were improved, too, and new stars began gaining fame and national prominence. Tom Mix had his own traveling circus in the late 1930s that toured from coast to coast in a highway caravan consisting of sixty truck-and-trailer rigs. The "Lion King" Terrell Jacobs and animal trainer Clyde Beatty, the famous clowns Emmett Kelly and Otto Griebling, Allen King and the Albert Hodgini Troupe all came into renown during that period.

Overall, though, the last years of the 1930s and the war years of the first half of the 1940s were not good ones for traveling circuses. The souring economic climate and madness of World War II essentially ended the circus experience for millions of children all over the United States. Only one or two traveling shows remained: the giant Ringling Bros. and Barnum & Bailey Circus, which had moved its winter quarters to Florida, and the smaller Cole Bro's and Clyde Beatty Circus, which bounced from wintering in California back to Indiana. Both struggled through an era that saw the Cole Brothers operation go bankrupt and be sold by January 1950.

Bought by the Otis Circus Corporation, the Cole Brothers Circus attempted another performance campaign in 1951 and paraded itself from its winter quarters two miles south of Peru, Indiana, through the heart of the city to the Wabash Railroad station on the city's north side. The financial reward of that campaign attempt was not enough to keep it traveling from location to location, and the tour was subsequently reduced to just a few weeks on the road. It returned to Peru, Indiana, for the last time and brought with it a sense of sadness that even a four-year-old could recognize.

That four-year-old was this writer, who, along with his mother and baby sister, was standing near the end of the iron trestle highway bridge over the Wabash River that circuses had crossed for over fifty years. The passage of the feather-bedecked horses pulling the gilded and brightly painted wagons was marred by the scream of the old steam-powered calliope, a sound that was pure torture to the ears of a little boy. And then, just as the tail end of that parade was off the bridge, two or three red trucks from the Peru Fire Department came roaring over that same bridge in response to a fire alarm—much like at the 1910 parade in Hammond.

A few years later, another attempt was made to put a traveling tent circus back on the road. I remember sitting with my father watching a series of acts in a one-ring big-top tent placed on an empty lot in Rochester, Indiana. It was an evening performance, and a very wet and windy thunderstorm was raging outside the tent. At one point, immediately after a powerful bolt of lightning struck nearby, the wind gusted so much that a side of the huge tent ripped apart and drenched the few of us who stayed to see the entire show.

For me, that truly was the end of the traveling circuses, although I have since been to a performance of the Ringling Bros. and Barnum & Bailey Circus held in a massive concrete coliseum. It is not the same up-close-and-personal experience as a tent show.

Warren A. Reeder Jr. also could not forget his disappointment at missing the 1918 performance of the circus. Fifty years later, when he was fifty-five and a successful Hammond businessman, he began researching the wreck of the Hagenbeck-Wallace Circus train, and his efforts eventually appeared in his self-published 1972 book, *No Performances Today*. In 1968, Reeder was a realtor with his own agency, a member of the Hammond Public Library Board, a member of the Civil War Round Table of Chicago and a founder and president of the Hammond Historical Society. Consequently, he had the resources and assistance of other highly capable individuals who could assist in his research.

Perhaps the most significant contributions came from the statements from eyewitnesses and participants to the tragedy that Reeder was able to obtain. One of the most vital came from the interviews he conducted with Oscar Timm, the circus train brakeman, just before Timm's death in the fall of 1968. Others who were there also shared their memories, and their contributions helped make Reeder's book an important piece in the history of the Hagenbeck-Wallace Circus.

However, the catalyst behind Reeder's literary work was the fifty-year anniversary of the wreck itself. With a dedication date set for June 22, 1968, the Hammond Historical Society and Warren A. Reeder Jr., in particular, began seeking individuals and accounts of the wreck as early as March of that year. Prospective contacts and some written accounts began coming back to Reeder in mid-April, and by the targeted June date, the dedication service was ready to be held.

Oscar Timm had been scheduled to attend the event as the guest of honor, but a sudden turn in his health forced him to undergo surgery three days before the event, and he was still recovering in a South Bend, Indiana hospital when the event dinner began. The long-planned celebration of his eighty-third birthday on June 22 kept Joe Dierckx at his South Bend home, too, but there were others in attendance who had been eyewitnesses or actually involved in the tragedy in one way or another.

Warren Reeder was the master of ceremonies for the event and played portions of the audiotaped interviews he had conducted with Oscar Timm, Joe Dierckx, Mayme Ward and others. Then he read the letters that he received from Alec Todd; Mary Marland, a student nurse who accompanied one of Gary's doctors to the wreck site and was then in South Bend at the Dierckx party; and a man named Huitz, who became a Hagenbeck-Wallace Circus band member that year.

Then it was time for the witnesses and participants attending the dinner to, one by one, stand and speak of their involvement and memories. Those who rose to the occasion included: Errett Martin, locomotive fireman on the first rescue-effort train to reach the accident scene; Ethel Howell, a nurse at St. Margaret Hospital who helped receive the injured who were evacuated from the site; Charles Strauch, an Ivanhoe Tower operator who reported to work in that tower at 6:00 a.m. on the morning of the wreck and relieved tower operator Hamilton Forbes; and Harold Wagner, whose father had been the yardmaster of Gibson Yard at the time and who tried to keep the worst details of the tragedy from his son. Finally, it was time for the dinner portion of the event to end and the next phase to begin. The historical society dinner was concluded and the meeting thus temporarily adjourned.

The next portion of the event could have been held at Woodlawn Cemetery, where so many of the victims of the tragedy were buried. The society chose not to do that, though, and instead reconvened the event at the actual site of the Hagenbeck-Wallace Circus train wreck. Consequently, a smaller crowd of adults, those who could physically walk the distance from the nearest automobile parking area to the location of the wreck, gathered along the old Michigan Central tracks at 3:00 p.m. that afternoon.

Guided by former tower man Charles Strauch, the gathering of men and women dressed in suits and skirts proceeded to the right-hand switch, where the second section of the Hagenbeck-Wallace Circus train began the transition from the westbound trackage and crossed over to the G&W line. Someone in the group (probably Warren Reeder himself) carried a large white cross covered in flowers, which was placed near the switch. Then, Reverend James Wiggins, associate pastor of the Christian Fellowship Church of Hammond, began a short but moving prayer service at the place where 86 men, women and children died and another 126 were injured.

Forty-one years after that service, during the gray and stark days of early December 2009, I went searching for the wreck location on my own. Snow had not yet covered the ground, and the winter absence of foliage allowed for a good search over the site, even though it was initially difficult to determine exactly where the key elements involved in the wreck are located. The most prominent feature of the wreck site, Ivanhoe Tower itself, is long gone, although the rods that once connected the switching levers in the tower to the switching gear that moved the rail transients are still there. Gone, too, are the massive telephone and telegraph poles that appear in the multitude of photographs taken at the scene in 1918.

The area houses are gone as well, and on both the southeastern and southwestern sections of land behind where the old tower once stood were sand and gravel pits. Even one of the east–west tracks on the old Michigan Central/New York Central right of way has been removed. The old Elgin, Joliet & Eastern Railroad tracks are still there and still cross the old Michigan Central at the same place they always have. The EJ&E is now the Canadian National Railroad, and the old east–west tracks belong to the Indiana Harbor Belt Railroad these days.

It certainly is an empty place now. There is no monument, no marker and no cross, and except for those old connecting rods, there is nothing left to identify it as the once-upon-a-time place where so many died. Perhaps that is the greatest tragedy of the Hagenbeck-Wallace Circus train wreck.

NOTES

CHAPTER 1

1. Records of the Indiana Adjutant General's Office, Indianapolis, Indiana.
2. *Peru Daily Tribune*, Circus Edition, July 15, 1986.
3. *Peru Republican*, July 15, 1892.
4. This remains a common railroad practice. Trains routinely are divided into sections due to length and weight limitations imposed by track conditions, motivation power available, the type of rail car, etc. Each section would have its own engines, caboose and crew yet would retain common timetables and track clearances provided for the entire train. In some cases, even the timetables and clearances would be issued to individual train sections, and only the stopping and destination points would remain common to all sections.
5. Adkins, *Circus Capital*, 12.
6. *Peru Republican*, August 14, 1903.
7. The circus was really a moneymaker for Wallace. It has been rumored that he made so much money on one tour that he shipped the coins to Peru in wooden barrels marked "NAILS" so as to escape possible theft. On another tour, he paid his help in nickels. It made them feel that their pay was larger.

8. Nancy Newman. "Untitled." *Peru Daily Tribune*, Circus Edition, July 15, 1986.

9. Adkins, *Circus Capital*, 18.

10. *Carl Hagenbeck v. Benjamin E. Wallace*. Charles E. Ballard, Ed Ballard's son, in a taped interview on December 14, 1971, in Peru, Indiana, flatly asserted that they were competitors.

11. By then, the circus had become the "big business" of Peru, complete with a two-hundred-acre farm for winter quarters and a five-acre railroad yard at the edge of town. The farm was originally that of Chief Francis Godfrey, leader of the Miami Indian Tribe. Everything was painted yellow, the Wallace stamp known to all. When Wallace died in 1921, it was expanded to encompass twenty-seven hundred acres.

12. *Lake County Times*, March 25–29, 1913. The author has this photograph in his family collection; it has been passed down from other family members who were survivors of that flood.

13. *Lake County Times*, March 31, 1913. The Michigan Central Railroad entered the state of Illinois in 1852 and made a connection with the Illinois Central Railroad south of Chicago. At that time, passengers and freight had to transfer to the Illinois Central to reach mid-Chicago. Several years would pass before the Michigan Central Railroad was finally allowed to operate on tracks into Chicago itself.

14. Adkins, *Circus Capital*, 24.

15. Fred Gollmar lived until 1966 and was almost one hundred years of age at his death. Gollmar, *My Father*, 45.

16. In 1924, city licenses were issued to six carnivals over a sixty-day period, and a Mr. E.J. Wilson had ten one-day "Medicine Shows" in addition. The Gollmar Bros. show put on a one-day "Menagerie Exhibit" in the north-side suburb of Robertsdale. The city took in a fee total of $1,000 in this period. Hammond City License Book, 1924.

17. *Lake County Times*, August 24, 1907.

18. Hammond City License Book; *Lake County Times*, August 2, 1910.

19. Hammond City License Book; *Lake County Times*, July 23, 1912.

20. Hammond City License Book, July 29, 1914. That morning an awe-struck reporter watched as 1,009 employees consumed over three thousand pancakes from the twenty-two-foot grill in the kitchen tent (always the first tent to be erected).

CHAPTER 2

21. Schoon, *Calumet Beginnings*, 45–60.
22. Marsh, *Michigan Central*, 87–88.
23. Moore, *Calumet Region*, 89–98, 179 map, 344–99.
24. A few farmers and sons of farmers did serve in either Illinois or Indiana regiments during that war, but there were not many. In fact, the entire population of North Township did not have enough able-bodied young men to fill its draft quota during the latter part of the war, and the other townships in the county were called on for additional manpower to make up the difference.
25. Moore, *Calumet Region*, 142–44.
26. Casgrain, "Memorandum," 2–3.
27. Bureau of the Census, *Ninth Census: Indiana, Lake County, North Township* (Washington, D.C.: Government Printing Office, n.d.), Microfilm Roll T-8-83.
28. Casgrain, "Memorandum," 5.
29. Bureau of the Census, *Tenth Census: Indiana, Lake County, North Township* (Washington, D.C.: Government Printing Office, n.d.), Microfilm Roll T-9-291.
30. Moore, *Calumet Region*, 147–60.
31. Marsh, *Michigan Central*, 202.
32. Currently, the small tower still stands on its original site, and it still has the light board denoting all switches and all tracks. The actual switching levers have long since been disconnected and removed, and attempts to save and relocate that tower to another site are still to succeed.
33. Casgrain, "Memorandum," 12–14.
34. A comprehensive account of the creation and interlinking of all the belt-line railroads around Chicago and its region has yet to be written. The Indiana Harbor Belt Railroad of today is the operation that either absorbed or inherited the many smaller attempts to interconnect all of Chicago's mainline rail carriers, and it was an 1896 outgrowth of the New York Central system.
35. Casgrain, "Memorandum," 11.
36. Moore, *Calumet Region*, 147–60.

37. Bureau of the Census, *Twelfth Census: Indiana, Lake County, North Township* (Washington, D.C.: Government Printing Office, n.d.), Microfilm Roll T-11-2.
38. Ibid.
39. Schoon, *Calumet Beginnings*, 114.
40. Moore, *Calumet Region*, 147–60.

CHAPTER 3

41. *Lake County Times*, June 22, 1918.
42. *Billboard Magazine*, June 15, 1918. The quote was cited in Reeder, *No Performances Today*, 14.
43. Holbrook, *American Railroads*, 282.
44. Interstate Commerce Commission (ICC), *Report*, 3.
45. White, *Passenger Car*, 240–44; Kratville, *Pullman-Standard Classics*, 1–3.
46. ICC, *Report*, 12.
47. Ibid., 9.
48. Ibid., 2.
49. Ibid., 3.
50. Ibid., 3–4.

CHAPTER 4

51. There is nothing that actually states that locomotive 8485 was a 4-6-0 "ten-wheeler" steam engine. I make this claim based on what is visible in the photographs taken at the wreck. The remainder of the information cited is contained in several pages of the ICC report.
52. ICC, *Report*, 7–10.
53. Ibid., 2, 7.
54. Reeder, *No Performances Today*, 95.
55. ICC, *Report*, 3–7.
56. Reeder, *No Performances Today*, 60.
57. Ibid., 61.
58. *Lake County Times*, June 22, 1918.

59. Reeder, *No Performances Today*, 60.
60. Ibid., 63.
61. Ibid., 67.
62. Ibid., 47–53.
63. Ibid., 53.
64. *Lake County Times*, June 22, 1918.
65. Reeder, *No Performances Today*, 51–55.
66. Ibid., 132.
67. Ibid., 67–68.

Chapter 5

68. Ibid., 56
77. Ibid., 69.
69. ICC, *Report*, 8.
70. *Lake County Times*, June 22, 1918.
71. Reeder, *No Performances Today*, 74.
72. Ibid., 75.
73. *Lake County Times*, June 22, 1918.
74. Ibid., June 23, 1918.
75. Reeder, *No Performances Today*, 59.
76. Data was taken from copies of Admissions Office, *Register of Admissions*, June 20–24, 1918. The copies were made from the original admission register now held by a local private collector. The copies are in the Hagenbeck-Wallace file, Suzanne G. Long Local History Room, Hammond Public Library, Hammond, Indiana.
77. Reeder, *No Performances Today*, 69.

Chapter 6

78. Ibid., 82.
79. Bundy, *West Baden Springs*, 125.
80. Ballard, *The Ballards*, 29.
81. Reeder, *No Performances Today*, 77.

82. Ballard, *The Ballards*, 96.
83. *Lake County Times*, June 26, 1918.
84. Reeder, *No Performances Today*, 112.
85. Ibid., 113.

Chapter 7

86. Lake County Coroner Report, June 25, 1918.
87. Reeder, *No Performances Today*, 99–103.
88. Ballard, *The Ballards*, 86.
89. Bradbury, *Circus Winter Quarters*, 7.
90. Charles Ringling passed away on December 3, 1926. Ballard, *The Ballards*, 88; Adkins, *Circus Capital*, 88.
91. Ballard, *The Ballards*, 114.

BIBLIOGRAPHY

Primary Sources

Admissions Office. *Register of Hospital Admissions for Mercy Hospital*. Gary, IN, 1918.

City of Hammond, Indiana. City License Books, 1910–1924. Hammond Historical Society. Suzanne G. Long Local History Room, Hammond Public Library, Hammond, Indiana.

Hagenbeck-Wallace Circus File. Suzanne G. Long Local History Room, Hammond Public Library, Hammond, Indiana.

Interstate Commerce Commission, in Conjunction With the Indiana Public Service Commission. *Report of the Chief of the Bureau of Safety Covering the Investigation of an Accident which Occurred on the Michigan Central Railroad at Ivanhoe, Ind., on June 22, 1918*. Washington, D.C.: Government Printing Office, 1918.

Lake County Coroner Report, June 25, 1918. Microfilm Roll # 5447. Office of the Lake County Coroner, Crown Point, Indiana.

Lake County [Hammond, Indiana] *Times*, March 20–30, 1913; June 18–26, 1918.

Peru [Indiana] *Daily Tribune*, Circus Edition, July 15, 1986.

Peru [Indiana] *Republican*, July 15, 1892.

Superior Court of Cook County, Illinois. *Carl Hagenbeck v. Benjamin E. Wallace*. Gen. Doc. 269, October 14, 1908.

SECONDARY SOURCES

Articles

Fenza, Paula J. "'The Day the Show Didn't Go On': Showmen's Rest and Woodlawn Cemetery." *AGS Quarterly* 26, no. 2 (2002).

Books

Adkins, Kreig A. *Peru: Circus Capital of the World*. Images of America Series. Charleston, SC: Arcadia Publishing, 2009.

Ballard, Charles Edward. *Charles Edward "Ed" Ballard: A Story of Determination, Self-Education and Ultimate Success*. Indianapolis, IN: C.E. Ballard Trust, 1984.

Barger, Ralph L. *A Century of Pullman Cars: Volume Two, The Palace Cars*. Sykesville, MD: Greenberg Publishing Company, Inc. 1990.

Bradbury, Joseph T. *The Circus Winter-Quarters in West Baden, Indiana*. French Lick, IN: Chamber of Commerce, n.d.

Bundy, Chris. *West Baden Springs: The Famous Health and Pleasure Resort*. Indianapolis, IN: Historic Landmarks of Indiana Foundation, 2007.

Gollmar, Robert. *My Father Owned a Circus*. Boise, ID: Caxton Brothers, 1965.

Holbrook, Stewart H. *The Story of American Railroads*. New York: Crown Publishers, 1947.

Kratville, William W. *Pullman-Standard Classics*. Omaha, NE: Pullman-Standard, Inc., 1962.

Longest, David E. *Railroad Depots of Northern Indiana*. Images of Rail Series. Charleston, SC: Arcadia Publishing, 2007.

Marsh, Nicholas A. *The Michigan Central Railroad: History of the Main Line, 1846–1901*. Ann Arbor, MI: Nicholas A. Marsh, 2007.

Moore, Powell A. *The Calumet Region, Indiana's Last Frontier*. Indiana Historical Collections, Vol. 39. Indianapolis: Indiana Historical Bureau, 1959.

Reeder, Warren A., Jr. *No Performances Today, June 22, 1918.* Hammond, IN: North State Press, Inc., 1972.

Schoon, Kenneth J. *Calumet Beginnings: Ancient Shorelines and Settlements at the South End of Lake Michigan.* Bloomington: Indiana University Press, 2003.

White, John H. *The American Railroad Passenger Car.* Baltimore, MD: John Hopkins University Press, 1978.

Unpublished Material

Casgrain, Wilfred V. "Memorandum on the Life of George H. Hammond, 1838–1886." Suzanne G. Long Local History Room, Hammond Public Library, Hammond, Indiana.

ABOUT THE AUTHOR

Richard Lytle is the local history librarian at the Hammond Public Library and an officer of the Hammond Historical Society. He has previously published two books on military history—*The Soldiers of America's First Army: 1791* and *The Old Guard in 1898*—and has been eager to write this book since taking on his post at the library eight years ago and gaining access to its collection of unpublished train wreck photos.